CHAKRAS
THE MAGNIFICENT SEVEN

Pathways to Higher Energy,
Happiness and Health

by
Paula Shaw, CADC, DCEP

After Midnight Press ♦ *Encinitas, California*

Cover Design by Sara Correia
Interior Design by Kathy Giangregorio

Many thanks to Casey Shaw for the title; to Erin Shaw for her diagram and her marketing savy and tfor her "eagle eye."

And to NavigatorPress for their generous assistance in preparing the manuscript file.

Paula Shaw Counseling Services
561 Saxony Pl. Ste 101
Encinitas, California 92024
Telephone: (858) 480-9234
e-mail: PaulaShawCounseling@gmail.com
www.paulashaw.com

The author of this book, Paula Shaw, has provided information and techniques to help you achieve clearing and balancing of the chakra system. She is dispensing neither medical nor psychological advice. The author and publisher take no responsibility for the manner in which this information is utilized, nor do they assume liability for any actions or for the results of those actions, which you may take as a result of the information herein contained.

Printed in the U.S.A.

ISBN 0-9716580-9-9

Second Edition Printing 2012

To my children,
Erin and Casey Shaw,
for loving me
and for being patient
with my absence and preoccupation
during this process.

To Mom and Dad, who gave me life.
And to the rest of my wonderful, brilliantly
funny family who love and support me always.

To Jeremy Kennedy
who inspired
a little book to grow,
and to Kathy Giangregorio
whose love, skill, and patience,
made it happen.

and finally,
To all of the Divine Beings
who assist me every day of my life.
My Humble Gratitude.

Get Access to Exclusive Content

for
Chakras The Magnificent Seven
Book Owners only!

PaulaShaw
CADC, DCEP

As a token of appreciation for buying my book please visit the link below and get access to my **Inner Circle** where you will have special VIP materials made available exclusively to you.

Get exclusive access to:

- ❖ My latest Chakra Balancing methods,
- ❖ Research,
- ❖ Webinars
- ❖ Client success stories
- ❖ Instruction videos

PaulaShaw.com/vip
Password: Chakra

Contents

The Seven Chakras

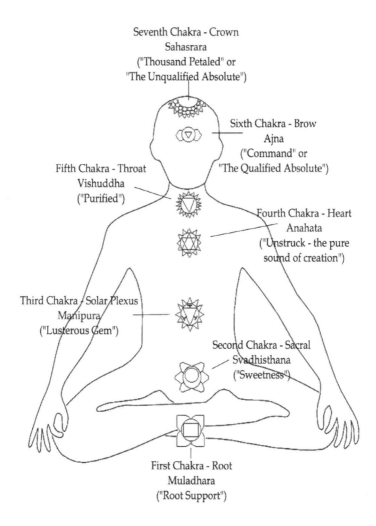

Seventh Chakra - Crown
Sahasrara
("Thousand Petaled" or
"The Unqualified Absolute")

Sixth Chakra - Brow
Ajna
("Command" or
"The Qualified Absolute")

Fifth Chakra - Throat
Vishuddha
("Purified")

Fourth Chakra - Heart
Anahata
("Unstruck - the pure
sound of creation")

Third Chakra - Solar Plexus
Manipura
("Lusterous Gem")

Second Chakra - Sacral
Svadhisthana
("Sweetness")

First Chakra - Root
Muladhara
("Root Support")

diagram by Erin Shaw

INTRODUCTION

THE CHAKRAS

The seven major chakras of the Human Energy System form a self-perpetuating spiral of energy. They are like mini tornados of energy, whose purpose is the reception, assimilation and transmission of vital life forces. Each chakra is a unique reservoir from which electromagnetic energy flows to nurture all parts of the body-mind-spirit system. These spinning vortices of energy are magnificent in both function and purpose, and are critical to our overall well-being.

The word "Chakra" comes from the Sanskrit and actually means "circular motion," though it is often translated to mean "wheel" or "disk." The chakras are typically depicted as lotus flowers, each resonating at different frequencies corresponding to the colors of the rainbow.

The Seven Chakras are positioned in the body in a straight line, beginning with the Root Chakra at the base of the spine, the Sacral Chakra in the lower pelvic area, the Solar Plexus Chakra in the stomach region, the Heart Chakra in the center of the upper chest, the Throat Chakra located at the throat, the Brow Chakra located on the brow between the eyes, and the Crown Chakra located on the top of the head. Interestingly, each chakra is located near one of the major endocrine glands of the body.

The chakras represent levels of consciousness that influence our perception of reality. They are the master programs that rule our lives, loves, learning and enlightenment. They are energy gateways through which we gain access to even greater states of consciousness. Beginning with the Root Chakra at the base and moving upward to the Crown, the movement of energy through the chakras is synonymous with the upward movement of consciousness. It is symbolic of the soul journey we undertake, going from the darkness of primitive, self-focused behavior, through the expression of the ego, on to a more highly-evolved loving perspective, and finally emerging into the higher states of compassion, wisdom, and enlightenment.

The chakras serve the parts of the physical body that fall within each of their areas of influence, providing the cells, organs, and limbs with the life force necessary for optimal functioning.   When that life force is unblocked and flowing freely between the chakras, the cells are in a growth state, and a healthy condition exists. When the energy gets blocked however, usually by negative focus and emotions such as greed, fear, and lack of self-love, the cells move toward a protection mode creating a general shutdown designed to preserve energy. When the energy gets blocked, stagnation, congestion, collapse, or over-inflation of the chakra can result. If prolonged, these undesirable states can become detrimental to the health of the body and the mind.   This is the reason that it is so important to process and heal life's challenging issues and remain positively focused. Everything on which we dwell impacts our energy flow and, therefore, our health.

Knowledge of the Seven Chakras, originally came to us from the Sanskrit tradition, which developed a rich, multi-layered explanation of the holistic nature of humankind. It teaches us that, in order to maintain a healthy, balanced life, we must not only heal physical dysfunction, we must also give attention to emotional, intellectual, and spiritual needs as well. Each of the Seven Chakras has an important role to play in achieving this goal. Each one resonates with specific mental, emotional, spiritual and physical issues we must heal and balance in order to create total health.

The Root or First Chakra deals with life force, vitality, sexual drive, survival issues, connection to country, family and tribe. It grounds us and gives us stability. It is the holder of our history and genetic identity. It is our foundation. It embodies responsibility, core energy, the drive to procreate, and personal empowerment. It impacts the lower regions of the body: the rectum, colon, sexual organs, perineum, base of the spine, legs, feet, knees, bones, skeletal structure, adrenals, lower back, fat, skin, and the immune system, as well as the little fingers and toes.

The Sacral or Second Chakra impacts and influences procreation, creativity, emotional balance, work, relationships, giving and receiving, working harmoniously and creatively with others, desire, pleasure, health, change, movement, tolerance, having enough, and assimilation of new ideas. It connects to: the reproductive organs, testes, ovaries, uterus, breasts, lower vertebrae, circulatory system, pelvis, hip area, appendix, bladder, prostate, kidneys, large intestine, and ring fingers and toes.

The Solar Plexus or Third Chakra deals with issues of personal power, the self, ego, personality, self-esteem, authority, the mastery of desire, self-control, how one functions in relationship to the world and how one feels viewed by the world. It impacts: the digestive system, stomach, pancreas, adrenals, upper intestine, gall bladder, liver, muscles, umbilicus, thighs, middle fingers and toes, and the middle spine located behind the solar plexus.

The Heart or Fourth Chakra is of course connected with love and the emotions. Divine/unconditional love, forgiveness, compassion, understanding, balance, group consciousness, oneness with life, acceptance, peace, harmony, and contentment are all attributes of this chakra. Its sphere of influence over the physical body includes: the heart and circulatory system, lungs, ribs, breasts, shoulders, arms, hands, diaphragm, chest, kidneys, and index fingers and toes.

The Throat or Fifth Chakra is concerned with issues of communication, inspiration, personal expression, creativity in speech, writing or the arts, the challenges of surrendering one's will to that of the Divine, and of dealing with issues of the unknown. It embodies such characteristics as integrity, peace, truth, knowledge, wisdom, honesty, reliability and kindness. It has energetic connection to: the throat, thyroid, trachea, parathyroid, hypothalamus, neck, esophagus, neck vertebra, mouth, face, teeth, ears, arms, hands, shoulders, all joints, big toes and thumbs.

The Brow or Sixth Chakra is the center of soul realization, intuition, intellect, inner vision, imagination, concentration, peace of mind, and insight. This chakra links us to our mental body, intelligence and psychological characteristics. Its influence on the physical body includes: the brain and nervous system, pituitary and pineal glands, eyes, ears, nose, the senses, the immune system and the base of the skull.

The Crown or Seventh Chakra is our connection with Spirit. It deals with unification of the higher self with the human personality, oneness with the Infinite, spiritual will, inspiration, unity, divine wisdom and understanding.

Humanitarianism, courage, idealism, higher consciousness, selfless service and perception beyond space and time are additional elements of the Seventh Chakra. It also has energetic connection with the central nervous system, the muscular system, the skeletal system, the skull, the cerebral cortex, the pituitary and pineal glands, and the skin.

✳✳✳✳

Although the chakras range from lower to higher and they resonate in accordance with those frequencies, I feel it is a mistake to extend this classification strategy into a statement about the order of importance or desirability of the chakras. While in the classic Sanskrit tradition, the teachings advise repression of the lower chakras in order to achieve higher states of consciousness, I tend to agree with the thinking of author, Anodea Judith (*Wheels of Light*), that all the chakras are equally important to our growth and life experiences. We would not be connected and whole without our roots, our sexuality and our power. Nor would we be complete without love, thought and spirit. It is the balance of all of the Magnificent Seven that creates health, vitality, wonder, confidence, love, high aspirations, serenity, creativity, contentment, and an awe-inspiring life experience. Understanding the chakras and working with them on a daily basis is the first step toward finding that balance and having that experience.

In the following chapters you will find a more detailed picture of each chakra. I find that the more I learn about the chakras, the more insight I acquire both personally and professionally.

One of those insights has lead me to working with the chakras in a way that I feel is extremely important.

This work involves energetically clearing the residue and negative influence of traumatic experiences that has gotten locked into the chakras. An in-depth look at this process is a major focus of this book. It will be discussed more explicitly in a later chapter in which we will deal specifically with the impact of traumatic experience and its varied manifestations. We will also explore a method for clearing and healing the destructive fallout resulting from trauma that gets stored within the chakras.

The chakras most definitely are the Magnificent Seven. They connect the physical with the metaphysical. They are reservoirs of experience as well as the beliefs, behaviors, memories, and attitudes created by it. Each chakra contains an imprint of every important or emotionally significant event experienced in a given life. They are vibrant, resonating spheres of life force, influencing the health of body, mind and spirit.

Use the knowledge provided in this book to create your own healing strategy. Find the chakra balancing techniques that appeal to you and follow through with using them each day. Don't try to do too much, it isn't necessary. One technique, consistently utilized, can do more to balance a given chakra than ten techniques inconsistently done. Use the techniques you enjoy and you will see results. They will enable you to create and maintain health and balance in the physical, mental, emotional, and spiritual areas of your life.

Chapter One

First Chakra

FIRST CHAKRA - Root
The Right to Life - "I have"

Sanskrit Name	*Muladhara* (meaning: root or support)
Location	Base of the spine or the Perineum
Gland/Hormone	Adrenals/Adrenaline, Cortico Steroids
Predominant Color	Red
Archetypes	Mother/Victim
Divine Association	Archangel Michael
Associated Deities	
Hindu	Brahma, Dakini, Ganesha, Kubera, Uma, Lakshmi, Prisni
Other	Gaia, Demeter/Persephone, Erda, Ereshkigal, Anat, Pele, Laka, Ceridwen, Hades, Pwyll, Dumuzi, Tammuz, Atlas
Sacramental Association	Baptism
Sacred Truth	*All is one.*

Qualities	Ability to manifest dreams
	Order
	Patience
	Security
	Stability
	Life-promoting energy
Element and Ruling Planet	Earth
	Saturn
Developmental Age and Life Lessons	1-8 years
	Standing up for oneself
Seed Sound	Lam (as in "mom")
Vowel Sound	O (as in "Rope")
Note	C
Music	Rhythmic: African or Native American drumming
Associated Sense	Smell
Emotion	Fear
Gemstones	Black Onyx
	Bloodstone
	Carnelian
	Garnet
	Hematite
	Labradorite
	Obsidian
	Ruby

Force	Gravity
Metal	Lead
Fragrances	Cedarwood Myrrh Patchouli Sandalwood
Herbs for Incense	Cedar
Flower	Red Lily
Essential Oils (Aromatherapy)	Curry Ginger Lotus Magnolia Musk Pine Vetivert
Astrological Association	Capricorn
Animals	Bull Elephant Ox
Foods	Proteins, Meats
Cord in Root Chakra Means	"I want you to help me survive."

Function: Survival

❖ The Root Chakra is concerned with the survival essentials that keep the physical body alive, such as money, food, shelter and clothing.

❖ It is based in Tribal Mind – Loyalty to family and to country. There is natural concern with immediate and extended family as well as family expectations, family legacy, generational traditions and beliefs. It also deals with race, social status, educational level, group identity, and survival of the species.

❖ It grounds us to the physical world and to physical experience, including sexual desire and lust.

❖ It embodies group force, group willpower, and group belief patterns.

Energy Connection to the Mental/Emotional Body

This is the foundation; the Life Principle. Emotional and psychological stability originates in the family unit and early social environment, forming the foundation of mental/ emotional health. This chakra resonates with feeling a sense of trust that the world is a safe place that will support us. It relates to producing results and to sexual drive.

When Energy is Balanced:

There is support and loyalty that enables you to feel safe and connected in the physical world. There is a tribal/ family identity and honor code. Bonding, security, stability, predictability, courage, empowerment, responsibility, as well as physical vitality, groundedness, the ability to nurture yourself and others, and a balanced drive for physical intimacy, is also present.

When Energy is Unbalanced:

You feel mental lethargy, "spaciness," and an inability to experience inner calm. There is difficulty maintaining employment or consistent living circumstances. You come from a base of fear, there is a lack of commitment and an intense need for safety, security, and material possessions. You are unable to stand up for personal needs and desires, and there is difficulty providing yourself with life's necessities, including balanced physical intimacy. This imbalance can be the result of childhood abuse and/or neglect, often leading to unfinished issues with parents and limiting beliefs such as "I'm no good at anything" or "I'm just not enough."

Energy Connection to the Physical Body

The Root Chakra connects to the legs, knees, feet, base of spine, colon, rectum, penis, vagina, urethra, perineum, bones, skeletal structure, skin, fat, adrenals, immune system, little fingers and little toes.

Health Issues

Sciatica, varicose veins, chronic low back pain, rectal tumors, cancer, osteoarthritis, obesity, hemorrhoids, constipation, degenerative arthritis, skin problems anorexia nervosa, knee problems, colitis, digestive or bowel problems, and irritable bowel syndrome, vaginal infections, sexually transmitted diseases, infections of the urethra, and impotence.

Chapter Two

Second Chakra

SECOND CHAKRA - Sacral
The Right to Create - "I imagine"

Sanskrit Name	*Svadhisthana* (meaning: sweetness)
Location	Lower abdomen between navel and genitals
Gland/Hormone	Ovaries/Oestrogen, Progesterone Testes/Testosterone
Predominant Color	Orange
Archetypes	Emperor-Empress/Martyr
Divine Association	Archangel Gabriel
Associated Deities	
Hindu	Indra, Varuna, Vishnu, Rakini
Other	Diana, Jemaya, Tiamat, Mari, Conventina, Poseidon, Lir, Haumea, Dionysius, Pan
Sacramental Association	Communion
Sacred Truth	*Honor one another.*
Qualities	Abundance Deservability

Qualities (cont'd.)	Pleasure
	Well-being
Element and Ruling Planet	Water
	Pluto, Moon
Developmental Age and Life Lessons	8-14 years
	Challenging motivations based on social conditioning
Seed Sound	Vam (as in "mom")
Vowel Sound	Oo (as in "due")
Note	D
Music	Flowing music
	New age music
	Chopin
	Brahms
Associated Sense	Taste
Emotion	Desire or Craving
Gemstones	Carnelian
	Citrine
	Coral
	Fire Agate
	Golden Topaz
	Opal
	Pietersite
	Rose Quartz

Force	Attraction of Opposites
Metal	Tin
Fragrances	Jasmine Rose Sandalwood
Herbs for Incense	Damiana Gardenia Orris Root
Flower	Tiger Lily
Essential Oils (Aromatherapy)	Bergamot Coriander Honeysuckle Hyacinth Musk Patchouli
Astrological Association	Cancer, Scorpio
Animals	Fish-tailed Alligator Fish Sea Creatures
Foods	Liquids
Cord in Sacral Chakra Means	"I need you." OR "Give me your emotional support, pay attention to my emotions."

Function: Perception of Other's Emotions

❖ The Sacral Chakra involves lessons related to creativity, emotional balance, sexuality, work, and healing ability. Known as the partnership chakra, it is the one through which we perceive other people's emotions (clairsentience) and through which we procreate. It also contains stored memories and emotions, it is the seat of the unconscious.

❖ It is the *sacred womb of creation*, the point at which the soul embraces the body. It is connected to the creative force that generates life, and all imaginative creations. Unlimited creativity from the universe flows into us through this chakra.

❖ It is concerned with the quality of relationships, the daily physical aspects of living, and understanding what is enough.

Energy Connection to the Mental/Emotional Body

This chakra resonates to our need for relationships with other people and our need to have some control of the dynamics of our physical environment. Energy shifts away from tribal authority to developing personal, satisfying relationships. Authority, other people, creative solutions, and money are all linked through the energy of this chakra.

When Energy is Balanced:

You are capable of standing on your "own two feet" but are also able to maintain relationships with others. There is a shift from "I" focus to "we" focus. You can be invested and committed, yet still able to recover from debilitating losses of personal relationships, property, career, and finances. When this chakra is balanced, the strength to rebel and recreate a life, when necessary, exists. Personal and professional power, talent, and the ability to make decisions is solid and firm. Second Chakra balance produces a person who feels attractive, is positively creative, vitally alive, and who is sexually balanced.

When Energy is Unbalanced:

You can have problems with money, blame, guilt, power, and control. There can also be blocked creativity, abandonment issues, incest, sexual and/or emotional abuse. Feeling disconnected from one's core, emotional instability, lack of commitment, and feelings of isolation are other aspects of imbalance in this chakra.

Energy Connection to the Physical Body

This chakra connects to the sexual organs, testes, ovaries, prostate, uterus, breasts, large intestine, lower vertebrae, circulatory system, kidneys, pelvis, hip area, appendix, bladder, and ring fingers and toes.

Health Issues

Impotence, frigidity, infertility, ovarian cancer, menstrual and prostate problems, reduced sexual desire, bladder and kidney disorders, fibroid tumors, reproductive disorders, allergies, hemorrhoids, pelvic/lower back pain, over-indulgence in food or sex, and exhaustion.

Chapter Three

Third Chakra

THIRD CHAKRA - Solar Plexus
The Right to Personal Identity - "I am"

Sanskrit Name	*Manipura* (meaning: lustrous gem)
Location	Between navel and base of sternum
Gland/Hormone	Pancreas/Insulin
Predominant Color	Yellow
Archetypes	Warrior/Servant
Divine Association	Archangel Uriel Archangel Michael
Associated Deities	
Hindu	Agni, Surya, Rudra, Lakini
Other	Brigit, Athene, Helios, Apollo, Amaterasu, Papa, Apis, Ra
Sacramental Association	Confirmation
Sacred Truth	*Honor oneself.*
Qualities	Confidence Freedom of choice Personal power

Qualities (cont'd.)	Self-esteem Self-worth
Element and Ruling Planet	Fire Mars and Sun
Developmental Age and Life Lessons	14-21 years Self-esteem, self-confidence
Seed Sound	Ram (as in "mom")
Vowel Sound	Ah (as in "father")
Note	E
Music	Powerful, strong, assertive music (Beethoven/ Wagner)
Associated Sense	Sight
Emotion	Anger
Gemstones	Amber Golden Citrine Howlite Jasper Labradorite Laguna Agate Morganite Sunstone Tiger-eye Topaz

Force	Combustion
Metal	Iron
Fragrances	Bergamot Vetivert Ylang Ylang
Herbs for Incense	Carnation Cinnamon Marigold
Flower	Golden Yarrow Yellow Chamomile
Essential Oils (Aromatherapy)	Bougainvillea Clove Frangipani Mint
Astrological Association	Aries, Leo
Animals	Ram
Foods	Complex carbohydrates
Cord in Solar Plexus Chakra Means	"I want some of your energy; my own is not enough." OR "I would rather operate on your energy than be respon- sible for running my own." OR "I want to control you."

Function: Personal Power/Self-Esteem

❖ Lessons related to the ego, personality, self-esteem, authority, personal power, energy, mastery of desire, self-transformation, humor, laughter, and immortality are all involved with this chakra.

❖ This chakra is instrumental to the forming of a "self," in the process of individuation.

❖ It is the body's distribution point for psychic energies, the seat of the intuitive voice.

❖ It is the power/control center. Solar Plexus deals with will, personal power in relation to external world, accomplishments, ego projections, vital energies, self-control, the freedom to be who one really is, authority and self-control issues.

Energy Connection to the Mental/Emotional Body

Solar Plexus Chakra is the personal power center, the magnetic core of the personality and the ego.

When Energy is Balanced:

You are able to maintain a balanced sense of self, generate action, and handle a crisis. You have self-esteem, self-discipline, self-respect, personal drive, and the ability to achieve desired goals by taking the necessary risks to attain them. When there is Solar Plexus balance, you possess the qualities of generosity, courage, confidence, ethics, and strength of character.

When Energy is Unbalanced:

You take in more than you can assimilate and utilize. You are oversensitive to criticism and need to be in control. There can be authority issues, conflict, low self-esteem, fear of rejection, rage, anxiety, intimidation, a lack of self-confidence, self-respect, and/or self-control. There can be difficulty with trusting others, fear of responsibility or of making decisions, as well as distress in dealing with aspects of the physical appearance such as obesity, baldness and aging.

Energy Connection to the Physical Body

This chakra connects to the digestive system, stomach, pancreas, adrenals, upper intestine, gall bladder, liver, muscles, umbilicus, thighs, the middle spine located behind the solar plexus, and middle fingers and toes.

Health Issues

Digestive problems, indigestion, gastric or duodenal ulcers, the eating disorders anorexia nervosa and bulimia, pancreatitis/diabetes, colon/intestinal problems, arthritis, liver dysfunction, chronic fatigue, addictions, hypoglycemia, allergies, and obesity, particularly weight collected around the middle of the body.

Chapter Four

Fourth Chakra

FOURTH CHAKRA - Heart
The Right to Love - "I love"

Sanskrit Name	*Anahata* (meaning: unstruck)
Location	Center of chest
Gland/Hormone	Thymus/Thymosin
Predominant Colors	Green/Pink
Archetypes	Lover/Performer
Divine Association	Archangel Raphael Archangel Uriel
Associated Deities	
Hindu	Vishnu, Lakshmi (as Preservers) Krishna, Isvara, Kama, Vayu, Aditi, Urvasi
Other	Aphrodite, Frejya, Pan, Eros, Dian, Cecht, Maat, Asclepius, Isis, Aeolus, Shu, Hi'iaka, Hina
Sacramental Association	Marriage
Sacred Truth	*Love is Divine power.*
Qualities	Acceptance Balance

Qualities (cont.'d.)	Devotion
	Emotional connection
	Forgiveness
	Love
	Sensitivity
	Sympathy
Element and Ruling Planet	Air Venus
Developmental Age and Life Lessons	21-28 years Forgiveness and compassion
Seed Sound	Yam (as in "mom")
Vowel Sound	Ay (as in "play")
Note	F
Music	Mozart and Bach
Associated Sense	Touch
Emotion	Love and Connection
Gemstones	Emerald
	Green Aventurine
	Jade
	Malachite
	Moonstone
	Rose Quartz
	Watermelon Tourmaline
Force	Equilibrium

Metal	Copper
Fragrances	Bergamot Melissa Rose
Flower	Bleeding Heart
Herbs for Incense	Jasmine Lavender Marjoram Meadowsweet Orris Root Yarrow
Essential Oils (Aromatherapy)	Amber Attar of Roses Yasmine
Astrological Association	Libra, Taurus
Animals	Gazelle Antelope Dove and Other Birds
Foods	Green vegetables
Cord in Heart Chakra Means	"I love you." OR "I like you." OR "I need you to love me."

Function: Emotional Power

❖ Lessons related to love and relationships come through the Heart Chakra, including self-love and the ability to nurture your self.

❖ Through this chakra it is possible to experience a "oneness" with life and connection with divine/ unconditional love. It is the chakra of emotional perceptions, love, affinity, forgiveness, compassion, empathy, openness and nurturing ability. It connects us with others through emotions.

❖ It is the central powerhouse of the human energy system. It mediates between the body and the spirit. It bridges the lower three physical/emotional centers to the three higher mental/spiritual centers. It anchors the life force from the Higher Self, and energizes the blood and physical body with that life force.

Energy Connection to the Mental/Emotional Body

This chakra resonates to our emotional perceptions, which have a much more powerful impact on the quality of our lives than our mental perceptions do. As children, we respond to life with intense feelings of love, compassion, confidence, hope, despair, hate, envy, and fear. In adulthood we hopefully express our emotions in a more stable, consistent way, with openness, honesty, and compassion. We recognize that the most powerful energy we have is love. When the Heart Chakra is open, you are able to receive love and give love to yourself, to people around you, and to family and friends.

When Energy is Balanced:

You will experience love, forgiveness, compassion, understanding, balance, dedication, hope, trust, empathy, acceptance, peace, harmony, openness, contentment, and the ability to heal yourself and others. You will show feelings appropriately with an open heart. You are affectionate and unconditionally loving, with clear, open, honest communication, and group consciousness.

When Energy is Unbalanced:

You can experience a repression of love, emotional instability, co-dependence, and melancholia. There can also be fear of betrayal, loneliness and the inability to commit and follow the heart. Issues with forgiveness, grief, a judgmental attitude, unresolved anger, hostility, jealousy, and criticism can also be present. Issues with self centeredness, resentment, and bitterness are likely to be prominent. A decrease in the love of life and an inability to give or receive love are other problematic aspects of this imbalance. If the Sacral Chakra in a woman has been closed through rape, incest, or abuse, she can't fully open her Heart Chakra until the wound has been acknowledged and some healing has begun.

Energy Connection to the Physical Body

This chakra connects to the heart and circulatory system, ribs, breasts, shoulders, arms, hands, diaphragm, lungs, chest, kidneys, and index fingers and toes.

Health Issues

Poor relationships, circulatory problems, heart problems (angina, congestive heart failure, myocardial infarction), high blood pressure, emotional instability, problems with breathing, asthma, allergies, lung cancer, bronchial pneumonia, breast cancer, upper back, shoulder, or mid-back pain.

Chapter Five

Fifth Chakra

FIFTH CHAKRA - Throat
The Right to Personal Truth - "I speak"

Sanskrit Name	*Vishuddha* (meaning: purification)
Location	Throat area – central and base of neck
Gland/Hormone	Thyroid, Parathyroid/Tyrosine, T1, T2, T3, T4, Thyroxine, and Parathormone
Predominant Color	Sky Blue
Archetypes	Communicator/Silent Child
Divine Association	Archangel Gabriel Archangel Camael
Associated Deities	
Hindu	Ganga, Sarasvati
Other	Hermes, The Muses, Apollo, Brigit, Seshat, Nabu
Sacramental Association	Confession
Sacred Truth	*Surrender personal will to Divine will.*

Qualities	Commitment to truth
	Communication
	Creativity
	Gentleness
	Integration
	Integrity
	Kindness
	Knowledge
	Loyalty
	Peace
	Power of the spoken word
	Reliability
	Truth
	Willpower
	Wisdom
Element and Ruling Planet	Ether Mercury
Developmental Age and Life Lessons	28-35 years Personal expression
Seed Sound	Ham (as in "mom")
Vowel Sound	Eee
Note	G
Music	Gentle music
	Sounds of nature
	Transcendent themes
	Mozart concertos
Associated Sense	Sound, Hearing

Emotion	Grief
Gemstones	Aquamarine
	Azurite
	Bloodstone
	Blue Topaz
	Celestite
	Chrysocolla
	Hematite
	Jasper
	Kyanite
	Labradorite
	Lapis Lazuli
	Pearl
	Purple Rainbow Fluorite
	Turquoise
Force	Sympathetic vibration
Metal	Mercury
Fragrances	Chamomile
	Myrrh
Herbs for Incense	Benzoin
	Frankincense
Flowers	Forget-me-not
	Iris
Essential Oils (Aromatherapy)	Frankincense
	Lilac
	Patchouli

Astrological Association	Gemini, Virgo
Animals	Lion Whale Wolf
Foods	Fruit
Cord in Throat Chakra Means	"I want to communicate with you."

Function: Power of Will

❖ This is the chakra of communication, of inspiration, of personal expression, and following one's truth. It is connected to speech, reality checking, hearing, intention, definition, and description.

❖ It embodies the challenges of surrendering our own willpower to the will of the Divine.

❖ Lessons related to dealing with the unknown also connect to Throat Chakra.

❖ It is the center through which you receive your "inner voice" (clairaudience - clear hearing).

❖ It impacts creative expression in speech, writing, and the arts.

❖ The Throat Chakra is connected to the ability to receive nourishment and to taking responsibility for one's personal needs.

Energy Connection to the Mental/Emotional Body

This chakra resonates fully, to the mental/emotional struggles that come when dealing with issues of the unknown, learning the power of truth, the freedom of choice, and releasing our personal will into the hands of the Divine.

When Energy is Balanced:

You understand that there is a bigger picture beyond the painful present. You have integrity, faith, self-knowledge, and personal authority. You choose that which is for your highest good and you make decisions with strength and commitment to keeping your word. You create beauty and harmony for yourself and others. You selflessly serve others with a sense that your relationships have connection beyond time and space.

When Energy is Unbalanced:

You are driven toward perfectionism and the feeling that you need physical beauty, wealth, position, or power in order to be significant. There is a fearful, anxious response in dealing with the unknown. Difficulty with personal expression, feelings, thoughts, and beliefs is prevalent. You have an inability to stand up for yourself, follow your dreams, or create that which is desired. You may be fearful of surrendering your power of choice to the Divine. A judgmental, critical attitude, and lack of discernment are also common.

Energy Connection to the Physical Body

The Throat chakra connects to the throat, thyroid, parathyroid, trachea, esophagus, hypo-thalamus, neck and neck vertebrae, face, mouth, teeth, jaws, ears, shoulders, arms, hands, all joints, big toes and thumbs.

Health Issues

Depression, shyness, communication and/or speech problems, stuttering, thyroid problems, swollen glands, TMJ (temporomandibular joint problems), teeth and gum difficulties, throat and mouth ulcers, scoliosis, laryngitis, chronic sore throat, raspy throat, neckache, thyroid problems, tinnitus, asthma, joint problems, colds, addictive over-eating, hearing problems and ear problems.   This chakra resonates with the power of choice which is involved in every aspect of life, including illness.   Therefore, all illness connects to this chakra because choice, whether conscious or subconscious, is an element of the Throat Chakra.

44

Chapter Six

Sixth Chakra

SIXTH CHAKRA - Brow
The Right to Clear Lucid Imaginary Thinking - "I see"

Sanskrit Name	*Ajna* (meaning: to perceive, to know)
Location	Above and between eyebrows
Gland/Hormone	Pituitary/GRH, TSH, ACTH, HGH
Predominant Color	Indigo
Archetypes	The Intellectual/The Intuitive
Divine Association	The Goddess Archangel Cassiel
Associated Deities	
Hindu	Shakti, Hakini, Paramasiva Krishnal
Other	Themis, Hecate, Tara, Isis, Iris, Papa, Uli, Belenos, Apollo
Sacramental Association	Ordination
Sacred Truth	*Seek only the truth.*
Qualities	Beyond duality Concentration

Qualities (cont'd.)	Devotion
	Discernment
	Imagination
	Inner sight and knowing
	Intuition
	Knowledge
	Peace of mind
	Perception
	Soul realization
	Visionary thinking
	Wisdom
Element and Ruling Planet	Light, Telepathic Energy Neptune, Jupiter
Developmental Age and Life Lessons	No age Emotional intelligence
Seed Sound	Om sound (as in "home")
Vowel Sound	(Not a vowel in this case) mmmm or nnnn
Note	A
Music	None
Associated Sense	Sixth Sense
Emotion	None; above the emotions
Gemstones	Amethyst Aquamarine Azurite

Gemstones (cont'd.)	Celestite
	Cerussite
	Clear Quartz
	Fluorite
	Iolite
	Kyanite
	Labradorite
	Opal
	Sapphire
	Sugilite
Force	None at this level
Metal	Silver
Fragrances	Hyacinth
	Rose Geranium
	Violet
Herbs for Incense	Acacia
	Mugwort
	Saffron
	Star Anise
Flower	Rosemary
Essential Oils (Aromatherapy)	Amber
	Rose
	Sandalwood
Astrological Association	Sagittarius, Pisces
Animals	Owl

Foods	None
Cord in the Brow Chakra Means	Someone is "in your head" thinking of you, or wondering what you think of them

Function: Power of the Mind

❖ Lessons related to the mind and psyche, and to purity of thought and action are related to this chakra.

❖ It resonates to the energy of our conscious and unconscious psychological forces.

❖ It is the clairvoyant (clear-seeing) center, intuition, personal vision, insight, and wisdom are embodied in this center.

❖ It is the chakra of visualization, imagination, and insight.

Energy Connection to the Mental/Emotional Body

This chakra links us to our mental body, intelligence, and psychological characteristics, as well as the unique combination of what we know and what we believe to be true. The facts, fears, personal experiences, and memories within our mental consciousness are also aspects of this chakra. The interaction of these components can lead to intuitive sight, wisdom, and spiritual vision. It is the energetic connection to visions, dreams, angels, sensitivity, perception, and charisma.

When Energy is Balanced:

You will experience pure spirituality, humility and wisdom, purity of thought and action, as well as surrender to the will of God. There will be strong intellectual faculties, the ability to evaluate conscious and unconscious insights, emotional intelligence, creativity, and intuitive reasoning. You will be truth-based, self-evaluative, open to others' ideas, and able to learn from experience.

When Energy is Unbalanced:

Nightmares, learning difficulties, lack of concentration, and hallucinations can occur. Your thoughts are scattered and negative and you are unwilling to look within. There can be fear of intuitive skills and knowledge, misuse of intellectual skill, and fear of being open to other people's ideas. Paranoia and anxiety, cynicism, and a refusal to learn from life experiences can also be present. You may have a fear of truth and reality-based judgments. There can also be an inability to value outside counsel, discipline, and truth, as well as the fear of one's shadow side. There may be limited self-awareness and a lack of spiritual understanding or vision. Being overly detached from the world is another negative aspect of this imbalance.

Energy Connection to the Physical Body

This chakra connects to the brain and nervous system, pituitary and pineal glands, eyes, ears, nose, the senses and the immune system, as well as the base of skull.

Health Issues

Mental confusion, eye problems, headaches, brain tumors, blood clots, neurological disorders, poor vision, glaucoma, blindness, deafness, spinal difficulties, seizures, learning disabilities, tension, lack of concentration, neurological disturbances, sinus problems, nightmares, senility, nervous behavior, and paranoia.

Chapter Seven

Seventh Chakra

<u>SEVENTH CHAKRA</u> - <u>Crown</u>
The Right to Spiritual Connection- "I know"

Sanskrit Name

Sahasrara
(meaning: thousand-fold)

Location

Top of head

Gland/Hormone

Pineal/Melatonin

Predominant Colors

Violet, Gold, White

Archetypes

Guru/Egotist

Divine Association

Christ within
Archangel Jophiel
Archangel Metatron

Associated Deities

Hindu

Shiva, Ama-kala (upward
moving shakti), Varuna

Other

Zeus, Allah, Nut, Enki, Inanna,
Odin, Mimir, Ennoia, Kapo

Sacramental Association

Extreme Unction

Sacred Truth

Live in the present moment.

Qualities

Beauty
Indelible connection with God
Peace & Serenity

Element and Ruling Planet	Thought, Cosmic Energy - Uranus
Developmental Age and Life Lessons	No age Selflessness
Seed Sound	"M" sound
Vowel Sound	(again not a vowel) Ngngng as in "sing"
Note	B
Music	None
Associated Sense	Beyond self
Emotion	None; above the emotions
Gemstones	Amethyst Clear Quartz Diamond Danburite Iolite Labradorite Lepidolite Moldavite Purple Fluorite Pyrite Selenite Sugilite
Force	None at this level

Metal	Gold
Fragrances	Frankincense Lavender Rosewood
Herbs for Incense	Gotu Kola Lotus
Flower	Lavender
Essential Oils (Aromatherapy)	Attar of Rose Lavender
Astrological Association	Aquarius
Animals	none
Foods	none - Fasting
Cord in Crown Chakra Means	"I want to control you." OR "I want you to follow my teachings."

Function: Spiritual Power

❖ Lessons related to spirituality connect here. It is our
   spiritual connector. It impacts our capacity to allow
   our spirituality to become an integral part of the
   physical life as well as a source of guidance. It is central to having an intimate relationship with the Divine.
   It is the chakra of prayer and meditation.

❖ It is the chakra of "knowingness," inspiration, or pure intuition; seeing the larger purpose in our lives.

❖ It connects to free will and ownership of the body.

❖ Attitudes, faith, values, ethics, courage, humanitarianism, and higher consciousness are all connected to the Crown Chakra.

Energy Connection to the Mental/Emotional Body

It houses the energy that generates devotion, inspiration, spiritual will, unity, divine understanding, idealism, selfless service, prophetic thoughts, transcendental ideas, spirituality, mystical connections, cosmic consciousness, wisdom, aspirations, and knowledge of truth.

When Energy is Balanced:

You will experience unification of the Higher Self with the human personality. You have a conscious rapport with, and faith in, the Divine. Inner guidance, insight into healing, divine wisdom, acceptance, unfailing trust and devotion are present. Selfless service without need for reward, serenity, and the ability to see the big picture are other aspects of Crown Chakra balance.

When Energy is Unbalanced:

You may have depression, sadness, strong ego, resistance to spiritual growth, alienation, obsessional thinking, spiritual disconnection, inability to trust life, and issues with

Selflessness and humanitarianism. There can be difficulty seeing the big picture in life as well as an absence of faith and inspiration and an inability to make decisions. Confusion, feeling shut down, fear of death, and hesitation to serve are other manifestations of imbalance in this chakra.

Energy Connection to the Physical Body

It is the access point for the life force, which pours endlessly into the human energy system from the Universe or God. This force energizes the body, mind, and spirit. It influences the central nervous system, the muscular system, the skeletal system, the pituitary and pineal glands and the skin. It also impacts the upper skull and cerebral cortex.

Health Issues

Depression, loss of free will, paralysis, bone cancer, skeletal problems, muscular system and nervous system diseases (multiple sclerosis and Lou Gehrig's disease), genetic disorders, fatal illnesses, brain problems, pineal gland disorders, skin problems, sensitivity to pollutants, chronic exhaustion, epilepsy, Alzheimers disease, senility, boredom, alienation, confusion, apathy, and an inability to learn or comprehend.

Chapter Eight

Chakra
Balancing

CHAKRA BALANCING TECHNIQUES

1. Sound Therapy (music and chants)

2. Color Therapy

3. Nature Therapy

4. Aromatherapy

5. Reflexology

6. Gemstones and Crystals

7. Meditation/Visualization

8. Altar Building

9. Physical Exercises and Yoga

10. Music

11. Chakra Touch

12. Massage

CHAKRA BALANCING

Chakras, are centers of Prāṇa, life force, or vital energy. Chakras correspond to vital points in the physical body (e.g. major plexuses of arteries, veins and nerves.)

The chakras are the power centers of the human energy system and act as pumps or valves regulating the flow of energy. These reservoirs of energy can best accomplish their function when they are in optimal condition.

When a chakra is balanced and producing maximum energy, it spins smoothly and rapidly. The areas of the body and mind that are impacted by it will be in a high state of functioning, and good health will prevail. When it is overactive, underactive, congested, sluggish, collapsed or over-expanded, it spins in an irregular way. When this is the case, illness or dysfunction can develop in the areas of the body and mind that are influenced by that chakra.

One of the ways we can know if a chakra is out of balance is through observation of the physical or psychological symptoms being exhibited. For example, a person with an imbalanced Sacral Chakra, may have difficulty in relationships, have money problems, or may be impotent.

There are many ways to balance chakra energy, and while we cannot explore all of them in depth, we will take a brief look at some of the most effective ones.

On the preceding page is a list of twelve categories of chakra balancing techniques. These particular ones have been chosen to offer a variety of techniques that could be easily implemented into daily practice. I suggest you survey them all and choose the ones you feel will best accommodate your goals and lifestyle.

1. Sound Therapy

This is a very effective, easy way to help a chakra to become balanced. Remember, sound is made of energy vibrating at a particular frequency. If that frequency is aligned with the frequency of a given chakra, then it will help to balance it. It is that simple. Each chakra operates at a unique frequency, which determines its colors and characteristics. In the information given for each chakra, in previous chapters, you will find the sounds that resonate with that particular chakra, as well as the musical categories that provide the correct vibrational frequencies.

The chakra sounds (e.g. "Vam" for Sacral Chakra,) can be sung or chanted anywhere, anytime, even while driving along in your car! The musical pieces can be listened to, at any point in your day. Listening while relaxing is best, but in an effort to stay reality-based, I will admit there would be very little music in my own life if I only listened to it while relaxing.

2. Color Therapy

Like sound, color vibrates at a very specific frequency, which determines the color you see. Every chakra has a predominant color that corresponds to its vibrational frequency. However, according to author Donna Eden, (*Energy Medicine*), a chakra is rarely just one color. The seven layers of each chakra can vary in color according to what is going on energetically within that chakra.

Looking at something that is the predominant color of a given chakra, or visualizing the chakra glowing a color, clearly and brightly, are excellent ways to energize it. You can also imagine yourself breathing color into a chakra that begins to whirl faster and faster with each breath. See it vibrate and expand as the color grows brighter and brighter. It can be very effective to surround yourself with the chakra color by wearing it or sitting in an environment where it exists.

Another visualization technique that works very well is to see yourself in outer space, flying in and out of a giant grid of each of the seven predominant chakra colors. This is even more powerful if done while holding both hands on that chakra. It can also be fun to imagine yourself being bathed in each chakra color. You can see it swirling around you, or see it as sparkling bodies of colored water in which you float and frolic.

3. Nature Therapy

Being in a natural area that resonates with a given chakra is another way to balance it. The environment, including its sounds and colors, will help to energize or relax a chakra. The environmental setting most helpful for each chakra is listed, but if being in that setting is impossible, visualization of the setting can also work very effectively.

First Chakra: Sit directly on the Earth, ideally looking at a red-orange sunset or sunrise, allowing the beauty and harmony of that setting to fill you and awaken your passion for life.

Second Chakra: Relax in a body of water, a lake or an outdoor pool, feeling yourself supported and soothed.

Looking up at a moonlit, starry sky can also allow balance of the feminine energies of this chakra. The combination of the above could be really powerful.

Third Chakra: Spend time in bright, radiant sunlight, feeling its warmth on your skin.

Fourth Chakra: Take a walk in any lush green setting, especially one that might include pink flowers. Noticing the feeling of the air on your skin is also helpful.

Fifth Chakra: Spend time outside absorbing the clear blue color of the sky. Also effective is any setting where blue water exists, especially where it reflects the sky. A lake, the beach, a wide river — all can be great sources of renewal for this chakra.

Sixth Chakra: Allow yourself to recline and relax and contemplate the deep blue starry night sky.

Seventh Chakra: Spend time alone on the top of a mountain or some other high place where you can experience magnificence and silence.

4. Aromatherapy

Listed in the chapter for each chakra are the herbs for incense, essential oils and fragrances that resonate with it. Put them in your bath, on your body, in a diffuser, or incense burner. Any of these methods will allow your sense of smell to help heal and balance your chakras. Combining fragrances with visualization or meditation is really powerful and will enhance the process.

5. Reflexology

There are points on the body that correspond with each chakra.   If you use a gentle circular massage on these points, it can be extremely helpful for chakra balancing. This is not a deep tissue massage; it works on the energy level, so be gentle. These are the points for each chakra:

First Chakra: A point on heel of the foot, slightly to the inside.

Second Chakra: A point directly above the inside heel but not yet at the arch.

Third Chakra: A point right in the middle of the sole of your foot, the arch.

Fourth Chakra: A point right on the ball of your foot.

Fifth Chakra: A point at the base of the big toe, where the ball of the foot meets the big toe.

Sixth Chakra: A point in the fleshy mound in the middle of the big toe.

Seventh Chakra: A point at the top of the big toe and second toe.

6. Gemstone and Crystal Therapy

Gemstones and crystals have a vibrational influence that is energizing or soothing to a particular chakra. The gemstone can either be placed directly on the targeted chakra, or it can be worn, or carried on the body. It is possible to balance one chakra using one stone, or you can lie down and place the appropriate stones on each chakra and balance them all at once. This will require about twenty minutes and can be combined nicely with meditation.

You may want to cleanse and energize crystals and gemstones before using them. There are many ways to do this. An overnight bath in salt water is great. If there is no ocean water available, you can make it yourself with a combination of sea salt and water. Setting them out in the sun for an hour or two can do the job as well. You can also clean them quickly by holding them under running water or with the smoke of burning sage.

7. <u>Meditation/Visualization</u>

Although visualization has already been discussed, let me say a bit more. Since we're working on subtle energetic levels, it is very powerful to combine the mind power of visualization work and the inner calm of meditation in our healing efforts. Remember the brain and the subconscious mind cannot differentiate between what is real and what is realistically imagined. Having a calm mind calms the body and provides the following distinct advantages: One can more easily sense where physical pain originates and "feel" where the chakra is out of balance. Also, when we are still, we are able to hear the voice of inner wisdom. Finally, meditation and visualization encourage the development of imagination and creativity. This is desirable and beneficial for people of all ages.

Here is a simple little meditation/visualization that I like to use. You begin by breathing deeply and relaxing each part of the body from the toes to the head.

"Visualize yourself standing in a 'Power Place' (wherever that might be for you). See your body surrounded by a translucent egg of light, of whatever color feels appropriate. Now see that egg of light become a brilliant, golden white, and allow that Divine golden white light to begin to flow into the Crown Chakra, activating and energizing it. See it light up in a beautiful shade of violet. Allow the light to enhance your ability to feel spiritually connected to the Divine and to the entire Universe. Allow the light to continue flowing downward and, as it does, see it light up and energize each chakra in turn.

Next, see a wheel of indigo blue light at the Brow Chakra begin to whirl, illuminating and revitalizing your intuitive and intellectual abilities. Now see the wheel of brilliant, sky, or turquoise blue, at the Throat Chakra begin to whirl, enhancing your ability to communicate effectively, express your will and deal with issues of the unknown. The wheel of emerald green at the Heart Chakra lights up next, illuminating your ability to experience and express your feelings fully, to give and receive love and compassion. Then the wheel of buttery lemon yellow at the Solar Plexus begins to spin, empowering you to feel a strong sense of personal worth and the ability to interact effectively and responsibly with the world. See the brilliant orange circle of the Sacral Chakra begin to swirl now, vibrating and resonating with your ability to be creative, emotionally balanced, and able to maintain quality relationships. Finally, the wheel of deep crimson red at the Root Chakra begins to glow and spin, connecting you with earth, family, and the ability to survive. Now, see every chakra whirling in a blaze of rainbow color.

Then see the red light of the Root Chakra extend downward, through your legs and out the soles of your feet, becoming roots that search until they find a spot in the center of the earth on which to anchor. Now, for a few minutes, allow yourself to feel the power of this energy flow, coming in to you from the earth.

Then allow the energy of all the light in you and around you to permeate and energize every cell. Feel the warmth of this vibrant, powerful flow of energy. Feel it in you and around you, maximizing your ability to create that which is desired in your life. Then, as if a part of you could step back and view your being, see yourself illuminated by the golden white egg of light around you and the seven brilliant colors of the rainbow glowing within you. Notice that the light pouring into the Crown, swirling through the chakras, then flowing into the roots, now anchored in the earth, has created a beautiful bridge. It is a rainbow bridge of light that connects you to heaven and to the earth, a bridge that allows you to reach for the heavens while having the safety and stability of Mother Earth. Feel the power of the limitless possibilities available to you. Feel the peace, feel the serenity, feel the glow. Know that all is well.

When you have had adequate time with the last part of this visualization, conclude with three nice deep breaths and open your eyes.

This meditation/visualization can be as short as five minutes or it can take twenty minutes or longer. It's up to you.

8. <u>Altar Building</u>

An altar serves as a tangible sacred space that is a physical reminder of the chakra on which you have chosen to work. It's a focal point for the energetic work you've chosen to do. The altar can contain colors and items representative of a particular chakra (e.g., red roses for the First Chakra, green cloth and pictures of loved ones for the Fourth Chakra). Many ideas for the kinds of things to include on your altar can come from the information given for each chakra in this book. You can also devise rituals   that involve the care of the items on the altar or the use of them during meditation. All in all, these activities will help you to be more mindful of the issues and growth opportunities concerning the particular chakra on which you have chosen to focus. Remember it's your space. There are no rules about how it should be. Make it meaningful to you.

9. <u>Physical Exercises and Yoga</u>

Movement in the physical body and in the breath is a very important way to activate or relax a chakra. Exercise in general is helpful. I have, however, listed below some specific exercises and yoga postures for each chakra.

	<u>Physical</u> Exercise	<u>Yoga</u> Posture
1st Chakra	Half-squat Lunges Toe Raises	Standing Forward Bend The Mountain Pose The Crow
2nd Chakra	Abdominal Curl (sit up) with a Twist, Pelvic Rock	Pigeon Pose Spinal Twist Triangle Pose
3rd Chakra	Upper Abdominal Curl Planks	The Bow The Tree The Cobra
4th Chakra	Shoulder Rolls Back Stroke Bench Press	The Sphinx The Camel The Cat Pose
5th Chakra	Shoulder Shrugs Push Ups Tricep Dips	The Bridge The Fish The Plough

| 6th Chakra | Eye Exercises (focusing on various points and visualizing color) | Palming Downward Dog The Shoulder Stand |
| 7th Chakra | Rubbing the top of the Head Hanging Head | Head Stand Tranquility Pose Lotus Posture |

10. <u>Music</u>

Music was discussed when we explored sound as a chakra balancing tool. The vibrational frequency and aesthetic value of music can make it one of the most enjoyable chakra balancing methods. The chapters describing each chakra list the kind of music that resonates with that chakra. When balancing a given chakra, expose yourself as much as possible to the kind of music with which it resonates. Feel free to let your intuition guide you to other musical choices as well. Combining the music with meditation can be a very powerful healing modality. However, if the only thing you have time for is playing music in your car, don't miss out on that valuable opportunity.

11. <u>Chakra Touch</u>

Physically rubbing the chakra with your hand is another way of creating balance within it. Contact with the hand allows the chakra to be exposed to the electrical charge of that hand. Bringing this new energy into the chakra will impact its internal state. In addition, rubbing in a left-right motion brings in the left and right brain. Rubbing in an up-down motion brings in top and bottom brain, and patting the chakra brings in back and front brain. Rubbing or patting a chakra can be especially valuable when working on clearing the emotional issues of that chakra.

12. <u>Massage</u>

Massaging the parts of the body where each chakra resides is a great way to energize or calm a chakra. You can also do a massage specifically for the chakras, rubbing each chakra in patterns of circles or infinity eights. This massage is done on the back of the body while the person being massaged is lying down. The massage can be vigorous and can last about three minutes per chakra on the lower chakras. However, when you get to the Throat, the Brow and the Crown Chakras, the massage must become very light, gentle, and brief. You may want to seal each chakra after the massage, by passing a lighted candle over it making the shape of a cross. Then move the candle around the perimeter of the body three times.

There are fingers and toes that correspond to the lower five chakras. These fingers and toes can be massaged any time you want to do a little bit of "Chakra Maintenance."

The correlation is simple to remember. Place the thumb at the throat and the other fingers will correspond with the four chakras below the throat.

Thumb or Big Toe	Throat Chakra
Index Finger or Second Toe	Heart Chakra

Middle Finger or   Solar Plexus Chakra
Middle Toe

Ring Finger or   Sacral Chakra
Fourth Toe

Little Finger or   Root Chakra
Last Toe

Chapter Nine

Chakras
Heal the
Wheel

CHAKRAS
Heal the Wheel

My exposure several years ago to the brilliant work of Asha Nahoma Clinton and her Energy Psychology system SEEMORG Matrix Work, opened my thinking to yet another function of the chakras. It appears that they act as "holding tanks" or "reservoirs" for the energetic disruptions and negative patterns created by trauma.

I have explored this concept and worked with it extensively through the Energy Psychology modality that I developed, *Conscious Healing and Repatterning Therapy (CHART)*. A critical component of CHART work is clearing the stored impact of trauma, from the various chakras in which it resides. This is essential to emotional well-being. Whenever we experience anything that disturbs us so much that the memory of it causes emotions such as shock, rage, grief, anxiety, despair, fear, depression, distrust, guilt, resentment and the like, that event has been internalized as trauma. These traumatic experiences form energy disruptions or rogue frequencies in the energy system.

If there is no opportunity to process the impact of the trauma and clear the system, these disruptions or negative energetic patterns will be held onto by the chakras. Each chakra becomes a "holding tank" for the kinds of issues that are particular to its area of influence. They get stored in the chakra and cause problems on two fronts. They create an energy drain that leads to imbalance within the chakra, and they become sources of unproductive beliefs, behaviors, attitudes and emotions, which will likely attract negative experiences that match them.

The chakra system has a powerful interrelationship with the subconscious mind. In many respects it seems to be analogous to it. We have been taught that everything we experience gets stored in the subconscious mind. So where do the chakras fit in? Perhaps the way it actually works is this: The subconscious mind is like the **hard drive** of your computer, where all the information that goes into the computer is stored. The chakras are like the individual **programs** that classify, sort, and retain specific pieces of information particular to that program's function and purpose.

Traumas around physical abuse, for example, are primarily held onto by the Solar Plexus Chakra. This can be validated through neuromuscular testing and by observing the kinds of problematic issues that appear in the life of someone who has been physically abused. Common issues we might see are: addictions, obesity, obsession with the physical appearance, chronic fatigue syndrome, and/or psychological issues, such as anger problems and difficulty with trust, abandonment, and rejection. Depression and lack of self-confidence are other common manifestations of physical abuse. All of these conditions are also symptoms of Solar Plexus Chakra imbalance (see Health Issues- Solar Plexus Chakra chapter). The above problems develop when the chakra is imbalanced and, in turn, create a set up for further imbalance.

In a nutshell, the degenerative process at work is this: trauma creates energy disruptions, which, if not processed and cleared, become stored in the chakras. The presence of these energy disruptions causes an imbalance in the chakra, which can lead to a myriad of dysfunctional manifestations. If unchecked, they will lead to further energy drain, causing the chakra to become more depleted and imbalanced. Can anything be done to stop this downward spiral? Yes. Simply put, we can use an energy intervention to clear the original negative pattern from the chakra, thereby eliminating the primary source of energetic disruption.

In **Conscious Healing and Repatterning Therapy (CHART)**, we do just that. We use an energy intervention to clear a particular negative pattern. In so doing, we eliminate its degenerative impact on the energy system. In the **CHART** methodology, much importance is placed on clearing the traumatic impact of experiences not only from adulthood but from childhood and adolescence as well. I feel this is critical because children experience so much of the initial trauma that occurs in a given life. Rarely do they get the opportunity to process and release the impact of trauma, so it gets locked into the energetic circuitry of their chakras and energy meridians.

A matrix of unproductive beliefs and behaviors forms around the negative energy pattern and becomes so integrated into the child's personality that, after a time, it is almost impossible to separate the child's personality from the traumas that initially formed it. Sadly, it is upon this damaged foundation that the psyche of the adolescent is built. That psyche becomes further damaged by the unresolved traumas experienced in adolescence. This, then, is the legacy that will be passed on to the adult. Is it any wonder that by the time we are adults we are fearful, neurotic, frustrated, anxiety-ridden, isolated beings, with a plethora of physical problems, no sense of wonder or awe, and little ability to live creatively?

Why is it that in adulthood, even when we do desire to be healthy and high- functioning, we have such difficulty manifesting that outcome? I believe it is because our Inner Children, a critical aspect of the psyche, still carry the energetic patterns of past pain and trauma. This keeps them stuck, imprisoned in fear and darkness, and restricted by their negative beliefs, behaviors, patterns, attitudes and emotions.

Let's return for a moment to the analogy of the subconscious mind being similar to a computer hard drive. We likened the chakras to the programs that sort and store the information on the hard drive. Now, taking this one step further, we find that within the programs there are files that sort and classify the information in even greater detail. These files are analogous to the sub-personalities of the subconscious mind, the **Inner Child, Inner Adolescent,** and **Inner Adult.** The contents of the files are the positive and negative events that took place during those developmental periods of our lives. When negative experiences occur and go unprocessed, their damaging effects have the potential to be destructive to the optimal functioning of the subconscious mind. Like computer viruses, they contaminate it with harmful data and create a state of malfunction.

When damage created by a virus causes malfunction in a hard drive, the procedure to repair and restore it would require searching out and deleting the harmful data existing in the programs and files. Similarly, if we want to repair and restore our "damaged human hard drives," (subconscious minds), we have to search out and delete the harmful data (traumas and negative energy patterns) existing in our programs and files (the chakras and sub-personalities). To try to create a healthy life without clearing the sources of the original damage, would be like trying to fix a hard drive without destroying the virus that caused its malfunction. No matter what method we employed, it would be impossible to accomplish the goal!

If we are to create the changes we desire in our adult lives, we must first clear the "harmful data" existing in the psyches of both the Inner Child and the Inner Adolescent. It is the outgrowth of the pain and trauma from the early years that blocks energy in the present and prevents us from living successfully. As a result, we become stuck, dysfunctional, unhappy, anxiety-ridden and vulnerable to mental disorders, addictive, self-defeating behaviors, and unhealthy relationships. However, if we clear the negative patterning of the past from the chakras and sub-personalities that retain it, we open up a space in which we can create the future we really desire.

If we are willing to take action to heal the wounds of the Inner Child and Adolescent, we can achieve success with movement beyond the pain and deadness that weighs us down as adults. We must, however, go back and begin the healing where the wounds were incurred. Caroline Myss describes this beautifully in her book, *Anatomy of the Spirit.*

> *"The "wounded child" in each of us contains the damaged or stunted emotional patterns of our youth, patterns of painful memories, of negative attitudes and of dysfunctional self-images. Unknowingly, we may continue to operate within these patterns as adults, albeit in a new form. Fear of abandonment, for example, becomes jealousy. Sexual abuse becomes dysfunctional sexuality, often causing a repetition of the same violations with our own children. A child's negative self-image can later become the source of dysfunctions such as anorexia, obesity, alcoholism, and other addictions as well as obsessive fear of failure. These patterns can damage our emotional*

and professional lives, and our health. Loving one's self begins with confronting this archetypal force within the psyche and unseating the wounded child's authority over us. If unhealed, wounds keep us living in the past."

Fortunately, we don't have to resign ourselves to the above fate. We have the tools and the knowledge to identify our traumas and heal them. On the following pages you will find lists of typical traumatic experiences particular to each chakra. Clearing and healing these issues will be transformational in your life. It has been in mine and in the lives of many clients, whom I have guided through this process.

I have created a simple method for clearing these traumas on the energetic level. You can use this method with or without neuro-muscular testing. I personally love muscle testing because it gives us definitive knowledge of whether or not an issue resides within us. However, if you find it difficult or confusing, you can do the chakra clearing work without it. I will, however, give you a brief explanation of how muscle testing works, in the hope that you might want to investigate this invaluable tool.

Muscle Testing : Clinical Kinesiology

Dr. George Goodheart, a Detroit Chiropractor, did most of the initial work with muscle response and activation of acupoints. He developed a system called Applied Kinesiology. This system was later expanded upon by Beardall, who developed Clinical Kinesiology. This is the basis of much of current Chiropractic treatment and the grandfather of meridian-based energy psychology treatments. Others who expanded upon and refined Kinesiology were Diamond, Thie, Durlacher, Ross, and Callahan. They, and many others, have contributed to the creation of the indispensable diagnostic tool that muscle testing is today.

Neuromuscular testing, according to one of its principal pioneers, Walter H. Schmitt D.C., is all about monitoring the excitation and inhibition of neural pathways. The strength or weakness of the muscle being tested is a reflection of the status of its anterior horn motor neuron pool. To explain it more simply, the physical body is an elaborate system of electrical circuitry (e.g. nerves, neurons) controlled by the brain. When you say or think something that is truth for you or that resonates with your subconscious mind, the electrical and magnetic fields around the body become stronger and strengthen the muscles. When something is not truth for you or you don't resonate with it, the opposite response occurs and muscles test weak. Our internal states and processes are recorded in the nervous system and muscle testing allows us access to them.

Neuromuscular Testing Procedure

Selecting the muscle to test is a matter of preference, however, when testing another person, the arm (deltoid muscle) is usually used. The arm should be extended straight out in front. Another position, that I prefer, is having the elbow resting on the arm of a chair or sofa, with the hand straight up in the air. The tester gently pushes the arm toward the body when testing. A light touch is all that is necessary because we are testing energy resonance, not physical strength.

- The person being tested should have their head positioned so that the nose is pointing straight ahead, but the eyes are looking down at the floor. This helps to access the subconscious mind.

- Have the person being tested say **"positive"**, or **"yes"** then push gently down on the arm. It should be easy for the person to keep the arm in the same position.

- Now have the person say **"negative"** or **"no"** and push again. This time the muscle should go weak. This is the desired result, but just to be sure of an accurate muscle check, do one or more of the following two tests.

- Have the person being tested say, "**My name is (say their name)**." The muscle should be strong. Then have them say a fictitious name and push down on the muscle; it should be weak.

- If this doesn't happen, enlist the help of the subconscious by saying, "**Subconscious mind, clear any reversals and correct polarization.**" Then try the test again.

- You can also test by having the person hold their other palm just above their head. On **"palm down,"** the test should be **strong**. On **"palm up"** the test should be **weak**.

When testing yourself, use the same testing method. However, it is awkward to push down on your own arm and get an accurate test, so here are some methods for self-testing.

The O-Ring: The thumb and index finger of one hand are used to make a circle. Insert the index finger of the other hand and try to break through the circle. This can also be done where one tries to stretch open the O-Ring with the thumb and index fingers of the other hand. Again, on positive, the circle will hold; on negative, it will break.

Middle Finger Push: Using the middle finger, try to push down on the fingernail of the index finger of that same hand, or vice-versa. A positive test will produce a straight strong finger. A negative test will allow the finger to bend or move.

Sticky-Smooth Thumbnail: The thumbnail is either sticky or smooth when rubbed by another finger. Tell the subconscious mind and the energy system ahead of time, that you want a smooth nail for positive and a sticky nail for negative. This can be reversed if you desire. Ask a question and check the smoothness or stickiness of the nail. The subconscious will make it work...try it. Amazing!

Experiment with each of these methods to find which ones are most comfortable for you.

TRAUMA CLEARING PROCEDURE

On the following pages you will find lists of traumas that are specific to each chakra. If you choose to use muscle testing, simply make the statement listed (e.g., "I was not heard,") then muscle check. If you get a **strong** check, your subconscious mind is resonating with that statement as a truth. It represents a trauma that you have stored within that chakra. If the test is **weak**, you do not resonate with this statement. It was not a traumatic experience in your life history and doesn't need to be cleared.

If you got a strong muscle response, or if you didn't muscle check but are sure that you did experience a trauma of this description, then you are ready to clear the traumatic pattern as follows.

1. Sitting or lying comfortably, breathe rhythmically and deeply.

2. Place both hands on the chakra on which you are working.

3. Close your eyes and cross your ankles, right over left.

4. Affirm your Intention to clear your chakra of this trauma pattern (e.g., "My intention is to clear my Throat Chakra of the trauma of not feeling heard.")

5. Then slowly repeat the statement you are working on, several times, silently or out loud (e.g., "I was not heard.") This is like highlighting what you want the energy system to delete.

6. Visualize the predominant color of the chakra as you say the statement.

7. See yourself as a child. Allow any pictures that need to come up to do so. Your Inner Child may be trying to communicate with you about what happened to him/her.

8. Do the same with your Inner Adolescent and your Inner Adult. If you are not a visual person, just say the words "Child," "Adolescent" and "Adult" in your statement (e.g., "My Child was not heard.") After saying the statement slowly, at least three times, go on to the Adolescent and the Adult.

9. This shouldn't take longer than a few minutes and may not even take that long. However, allow whatever should happen. Sometimes a flood of emotion might come up, and that's perfectly normal. Sometimes you will see pictures of events you haven't thought about in years. Allow this communication with your inner selves to take place.

10. When the process is finished, repeat the statement and muscle test again (if you are using muscle testing). This time you should test clear, or weak when you say the statement (e.g., "I was not heard.") The weak muscle test indicates that you no longer resonate with this statement as truth. The trauma has been cleared. (If you are not muscle testing, see if you notice some kind of energetic shift when you think about the statement now.)

11. If you don't notice a shift, or if you did not get a weak test, then repeat steps 1-10.

12. Once you have gotten a weak or clear test, you are ready to install a present tense, positive statement using the same protocol. This can be the opposite of the negative one, or be creative and state the ideal condition you want to exist. (e.g. "I was not heard" could become "I am heard and respected.") This time after doing steps 1 through 4 repeat the positive statement seeing yourself as Child, Adolescent and Adult.

Once you have completed the process, check off that statement and go on to the next one. That's it. It is a simple process that you can easily do alone. Clear a few issues every day, or clear a whole chakra at one time if it feels comfortable.

Honor your body and energy system, however, don't push yourself too hard. I would never clear more than one chakra at a time. I even like to ask before each statement, "Is it okay to clear another trauma?" Then muscle test. If you get a strong muscle (yes), then proceed. If you get a weak muscle (no), then honor that request and stop.

Sometimes people experience a "chakra clearing reaction" after doing this work (e.g., leg pain eliminated after clearing the Root Chakra, or amplified emotions after clearing the Heart Chakra). If something like that happens, relax and know that it is part of the cleansing, healing process. Most of the reactions you will experience will be very positive, but if you should experience something unpleasant, know that it is temporary.

Feel free to clear trauma statements that may not be on the lists in this book. These may be even more powerful for you than the ones I have created. Remember, set an intention to heal your trauma wounds and then work on clearing each chakra until you have completed all seven. It doesn't matter how long the process takes, it just matters that you complete it. You will find that this small investment of time will be absolutely transformative in your life.

On the following pages you will find the lists of common traumas that I have identified.

FIRST CHAKRA TRAUMAS

◊ I was neglected.

◊ I was not safe.

◊ I was deprived.

◊ I was not comforted.

◊ I was sexually abused.

◊ My needs were not met.

◊ I was hungry.

◊ I was cold.

◊ I was taken forcefully.

◊ I was shamed during potty training.

◊ The life of a loved one was threatened.

◊ My life was threatened.

◊ I was defenseless.

◊ I was wounded by racial prejudice.

◊ I was abandoned and vulnerable.

◊ I was not allowed to become independent.

◊ I was overly protected.

◊ I had no stability.

◊ I wasn't nurtured.

◊ I had no financial security.

◊ There was no one capable of caring for me properly.

◊ I always had to be the parent.

◊ There wasn't adequate food and shelter.

◊ No one was there.

◊ My Government wasn't to be trusted.

◊ The rug was constantly pulled out from under me.

SECOND CHAKRA TRAUMAS

◊ I was abused by my siblings

◊ I was always uncomfortable with others

◊ I was creatively abused.

◊ I was sexually embarrassed.

◊ I was sexually shamed.

◊ I was confused about my sexuality.

◊ I was sexually teased.

◊ I was sexually criticized.

◊ I was creatively blocked.

◊ I was not allowed to be creative.

◊ I was not able to live creatively.

◊ I was creative but perceived as weird.

◊ I didn't feel connected to anyone.

◊ I wasn't allowed to be my own person.

◊ I wasn't comfortable with my sexuality.

◊ I was exposed to sexuality before I was ready.

◊ I was taught that my sexuality offended God.

◊ I was shamed during puberty.

◊ I was unattractive.

◊ No one wanted to be with me.

◊ I was never asked out for a date.

◊ I was sexually numb.

◊ My body always seemed different from the bodies of others.

◊ I was never able to attract a partner.

◊ I was unable to receive pleasure..

THIRD CHAKRA TRAUMAS

◊ I was invaded.

◊ I was attacked.

◊ I was hated.

◊ I was overly controlled.

◊ I was crushed.

◊ I was broken.

◊ I was manipulated.

◊ I was victimized.

◊ I was constantly watched.

◊ I was removed from everything familiar.

◊ I was not allowed to have boundaries.

◊ I was exploited and used.

◊ I was not allowed to be powerful.

◊ I was not allowed to have my own identity.

◊ I was not allowed to stand up for myself.

◊ I was physically abused.

◊ I was physically hurt.

◊ I was physically tortured.

◊ I was physically shamed.

◊ I was physically inadequate.

◊ I was physically criticized.

◊ I was never picked for a team.

◊ I was told every move to make.

◊ I was not respected.

◊ I was not allowed to individuate.

◊ I could never fulfill my goals and dreams.

FOURTH CHAKRA TRAUMAS

◊ I felt unloved.

◊ I felt rejected.

◊ I felt humiliated.

◊ I felt ignored.

◊ I felt shamed.

◊ I felt teased.

◊ I felt unappreciated.

◊ I was loved conditionally.

◊ I wasn't allowed to love myself.

◊ I was betrayed.

◊ I felt terrified.

◊ I was emotionally cold.

◊ I felt emotionally hungry.

◊ I felt abandoned.

◊ I felt constantly angry.

◊ I felt emotionally crushed.

◊ I felt judged.

◊ I was frustrated.

◊ I was miserable.

◊ I was constantly afraid.

◊ I was constantly anxious.

◊ I was constantly depressed.

◊ I always felt less than.

◊ I wasn't able to trust.

◊ I was unable to love.

◊ I was sick with grief.

FIFTH CHAKRA TRAUMA S

◊ I was not heard.

◊ I was shamed.

◊ I was teased and couldn't speak up for myself.

◊ I didn't know what was going to happen next.

◊ I was not allowed to speak my truth.

◊ I was not allowed to be expressive.

◊ I was not allowed to be free.

◊ I was not allowed to be assertive.

◊ I was not allowed to speak about certain subjects.

◊ I was not allowed to express anything negative.

◊ I was not allowed to express my anger.

◊ I was unable to stand up for myself.

◊ I was afraid to surrender my power to God.

◊ I was terrified to speak in public.

◊ I was afraid to speak to persons in authority.

◊ I was afraid to speak my feelings.

◊ I was afraid to speak my truth.

◊ I was afraid that "God's will" would not be my will.

◊ I was afraid of the unknown.

◊ I was afraid to express my beliefs.

◊ I was afraid to express my thoughts.

◊ I couldn't speak a painful truth to someone I loved.

◊ I couldn't "swallow" a painful truth.

◊ I didn't know how to tell my mother/father about…

◊ I didn't know how to tell my child about…

◊ I didn't know how to tell my partner/spouse about…

SIXTH CHAKRA TRAUMAS

◊   I couldn't stop obsessing and worrying.

◊   I was called slow.

◊   I was criticized for my performance in school.

◊   I didn't feel normal.

◊   No one believed in me.

◊   I wasn't understood.

◊   I wasn't allowed to be intellectually free.

◊   I was psychologically abused.

◊   I was psychologically tortured.

◊   I was psychologically hurt.

◊   I was psychologically shamed.

◊   I was psychologically teased.

◊   I was taught not to trust my intuition.

◊   I couldn't think clearly.

◊   I couldn't stay focused.

◊   I couldn't stop thinking and allow sleep.

◊   I couldn't stop my fearful thoughts.

◊   I was terrified of my dark side.

◊   I was never smart enough.

◊   I couldn't think quickly.

◊   I was shamed for my thoughts.

◊   I was shamed for my intuition.

◊   My thoughts were always negative.

◊   I couldn't see anyone else's point of view.

◊   I was convinced I was not smart.

SEVENTH CHAKRA TRAUMAS

◊ I was spiritually abused.

◊ I was spiritually hurt.

◊ I was spiritually shamed.

◊ I was spiritually criticized.

◊ I was spiritually manipulated.

◊ I was spiritually confused.

◊ I was spiritually afraid.

◊ I was spiritually dead.

◊ I was spiritually disconnected.

◊ I didn't feel the existence of God.

◊ I was kept away from god.

◊ I was depressed.

◊ I was demoralized.

◊ I was unable to make a decision.

◊ I had no faith.

◊ I felt abandoned by God.

◊ I didn't feel the existence of God.

◊ I hated God.

◊ I felt unseen by God.

◊ I felt unheard by God.

◊ I felt God hated me.

◊ I didn't trust that a spiritual connection existed.

◊ I had no trust.

◊ I didn't feel loved by God.

◊ I was afraid of spirituality.

Chapter Ten

Etheric
Chakra
Cords

ETHERIC CHAKRA CORDS

Etheric Chakra Cords are lines of energy that usually run between the chakras of two people. They exist on the etheric or energetic plane and are essentially a request for energetic attention. These cords can be seen by clairvoyant people and often look like hoses or tubes. They can be thick or thin, smooth or rough, twisted and tough, or delicate and fragile. This is usually determined by the nature of the relationship that is involved.

Cordings are a very common occurrence, they happen all the time. People pass cords back and forth with little awareness of the process and no damaging effects. In fact, cords can be beneficial because they allow us a means of having strong connections with others. Some cordings are natural and desirable like the First and Fourth Chakra cordings that often exist between mother and child. This connection creates a strong bond that will insure the baby's survival. Another desirable connection is the Second and Fourth Chakra cording that exists in the early stages of romantic love. This cording assures sexual attraction, connection and, of course, love. If the relationship is healthy, a cording can be a means of exchanging energy that can be mutually beneficial. This state might last or it might shift as the relationship matures. Sometimes at that point the cords naturally disengage as security, individuation, and personal boundaries evolve. If the relationship is unhealthy, however, and one of the partners is exceptionally needy, the cording becomes undesirable, developing into a means through which the needy partner siphons energy from the other. This puts the stronger partner at risk for becoming energetically drained and detrimentally vulnerable on a variety of levels.

In each of the chakra chapters I have listed what a cord in that chakra represents as an emotional message. In situations where a cord is created by fear and need, a disempowered state will evolve and the message will be needy or negative. For example, in such a circumstance, a cord in the First Chakra could mean, "I need you to survive." Or "I want you to help me survive." A cord in the Third Chakra could mean, "I need you to feel I exist."

Some of the relationships where we most commonly find etheric cordings are those between siblings, parents and children, ex-lovers or ex-spouses, and between current lovers and spouses. Any strong relationship can create cord connections between the people involved. This also includes relationships with circumstances and places (e.g., home, office, a special geographical place). All of these relationships can become fertile ground for etheric cordings, which can either be positive or negative, depending on whether or not need and fear are part of the equation.

In ideal circumstances, energetic cordings have a balanced exchange of energy. When this is the case we don't have much awareness of the cords because they are working for us in a positive way. It is the cords created from a disempowered state that are undesirable and need to be removed. We know when these are present because the manifestations of them are readily apparent. These cords lower the vibration of the chakra that is being energetically drained, causing the person to feel tired, anxious, obsessive, depressed, inadequate, disempowered, etc... Other manifestations of negative cordings could be, that you can't stop thinking about someone, needing someone, desiring someone, grieving someone, hating someone, or feeling threatened by someone. If there is someone in whose presence you can never seem to think straight, express yourself well, or stand up for your rights, this is probably the result of an etheric cording. These and other similar feelings and experiences are disempowering and, therefore, undesirable. In such situations it is advisable to proceed with cord removal.

Although some people can see or sense that they have etheric cords, most people can't. I have found that it works very well to use Neuromuscular Testing to ask the energy system if you have been corded, and where. The methods and rationale for muscle testing were previously given, (See pages 83-85). One of the most important advantages of using muscle testing is that it tests subtle energy states. Energetic cords are subtle energies and are not visible to the average person's eye, but they are very real and very powerful. I have had clients whose lives and relationships completely changed after cord removal was performed. It is easy to use muscle testing to find out if, and where you are corded. I also like to use it to help me decide what method to use to remove the cords. You will find several methods described later in this chapter. It is important to reiterate here that we can be corded with places, things and even the deceased. These kinds of cordings prevent us from expressing our true selves and living fully.

To do the testing, just sit comfortably and ask "Am I corded to...?" Then muscle test. If you get a strong response meaning, 'yes,' start with the Root Chakra and muscle check each one to see which have cords. (e.g. "I am corded to Jim at the Root Chakra.") Once you have gathered this information, you are ready to remove the cords. Several methods for cord removal are suggested in this the chapter. Don't worry, completing this task won't mean that relationship will end, or that you will no longer have feelings for the other person. It will simply change the energy-draining, fear-based parts of the relationship. This will either make it easier to let go of the relationship, or it will put the relationship on a new footing in which both parties are functioning optimally on their own energy.

Etheric Cord Removal

There are many ways to remove cords. You can have a healing professional such as a Reiki Master clear and remove them, or you can very easily do it yourself. The following are a variety of ways to do this.

Cutting the Cords: After getting yourself into a relaxed state, visualize the corded chakra. See the chakra's color, the more brilliant the better. Now see the cord in the chakra. Get a sense of what it looks like, its color, its texture, etc. Then see yourself holding a sharp cutting instrument like a knife, scissors, or sword. Affirm your intention to cut the cords so that you can regain your full energy and freedom. As you cut through the cord say:

> *"I cut this cord to free myself and to free you. I reclaim my light. I reclaim my power. I release you to reclaim your light and power. I do this in the spirit of love - for you, and for myself."*

Once you have cut the cord, do with it what seems appropriate. It is nice to send it back to the person from which it came in a loving way: in a rose, a crystal heart or some other symbol of love. However, it may feel more appropriate to fling it away or see it turn into sparkles of light that blow away. This is up to you. There is no right or wrong way. If a forceful, powerful ending would be more appropriate for your healing, do not feel required to end it in a gentle way. Remember at all times that this is your process for your healing. Do what feels right to you.

Removing Cords: Deedre Diemer suggests removing cords gently and lovingly, (*The ABC's of Chakra Therapy.*) I have adapted a method she uses, making a few changes.

Again visualize the corded chakra and see it with as much detail as possible. Now take hold of the cord with both hands. (You can physically do this or visualize it.) Slowly turn the cord to loosen it. When it seems appropriate to do so, begin to gently pull it out so as not to tear a hole in the chakra. See the cord leaving the chakra. See it as clearly as possible. Observe the color, the texture, and the strength. Sometimes this will give you valuable information about the relationship that created it. As in the prior method, it is advisable, as you are removing the cord, to state the following affirmation:

> *"I remove this cord to free myself and to free you. I reclaim my light. I reclaim my power. I release you to reclaim your light and power. I do this in the spirit of love - for you, and for myself."*

After you have slid the cord out, tie a knot in it or place it in a container of some kind (an earthen jar, a crystal, a flower, etc.) and fling it out into the universe. Again, if it is your preference to do so, hand it back to the other person in a kind, loving way. Then place your hand over the hole in the chakra and heal it with white light.

Angel Assistance with Cord Removal : Doreen Virtue (*Chakra Clearing,*) tells us that the easiest, quickest way to cut etheric cords is by calling upon Archangel Michael, whose primary role it is to clear away all dark energy. Just ask him to come to your side and clear away all cords that are draining you. You should notice an immediate increase in energy and peacefulness. You can also call on Archangel Raphael, the healer. His beautiful green, glowing light will wrap around each chakra, clearing it of any cords and healing it of any anxiety, stress, guilt or fear. Just call upon Raphael and ask him to enter your body and clear it of any imbalances or negative energy, and it is done.

The Blue Room Technique : This is a method that I have developed and used very successfully. A wonderful spiritual teacher named Tara gave me the idea years ago. I took the basic concept and adapted it for a cord removal technique. It encompasses a powerful setting, a strong affirmation and clear action.

Picture yourself in a blue room, the more brilliant the color, the better. In the room are two chairs. The person with whom you are corded is sitting in one of the chairs. You walk over and sit down in the other chair facing that person. See the cord or cords running between the two of you as clearly as possible. Then, for each cord, look the person in the eyes and say:

> *"Any sexual, creative, energetic, competitive, or co-*
> *dependent promises I have made to you in this life or*
> *in any other, I relinquish at this time with love. I*
> *reclaim my light; I reclaim my power to be co-creator*

in heaven and on earth. Any light or power I have taken from you I give back at this time with love."

Then gently twist and remove the cord. Tie a knot in the end of it and hand it to the other person, either gently or forcefully, depending on what your needs are and on what feels appropriate. Say anything else you may need to communicate, then place your hand over the hole that has been left and heal it with white light. You may give the other person some kind of gesture of love if you desire. Then get up out of your chair and leave the room, closing the door behind you.

If there is more than one cord, remove all the cords using this process before you leave the room.

Burning the Cords: A spiritual teacher named Elizabeth Medearis, taught me this last method. Find yourself sitting in any setting that seems appropriate and desirable to you. Across from you is the person with whom you are corded. See the etheric cords running between you. Observe as much detail about them as possible. Then, in a loving spirit, build a bonfire between you. As the fire burns more and more brightly, it destroys the etheric cords. There is no danger to either person from this fire. It is a cool laser-like white heat, whose only incendiary target, is the chakra cords. While this is happening you can look the other person in the eyes and talk to them if you desire. I would add to anything that you say, this affirmation formerly stated in other methods:

"I remove this cord to free myself and to free you. I reclaim my light. I reclaim my power. I release you to reclaim your light and power. I do this in the spirit of love - for you, and for myself."

When the cord is burned, the fire will die out, and you can use white light to heal the hole in your chakra. Then end the interaction in any manner that feels appropriate to you. While ending it in a loving manner might seem the most desirable way, it is more important that you be genuine. End it in whatever way you feel you need to.

Etheric cords are only a problem if we have no awareness of their existence or how to remove them. Having this knowledge, however, you can take the necessary steps to free yourself and reclaim your energy. Remember that cord removal will not, of itself, end the relationship or your feelings for the other person involved. It will, however, make it easier to end a relationship, if that is what is desired. If not, it will simply shift the dysfunctional, fear-based aspects of the relationship so that it can become healthy and balanced.

Cord removal, like all chakra work, requires three elements: awareness, intention, and action. These three elements, when consciously employed, can yield amazing results. They can open the door to impacting the body, mind, and spirit system in a powerful, positive way.

Chapter Eleven

Case Histories

CASE HISTORIES

The following stories are examples of how people have used the information in this book to balance their chakras and heal themselves on the physical, spiritual, mental, and emotional levels of their lives.

While it is true that certain issues are specific to a given chakra, I feel that it is critical to adopt a holistic approach to chakra balancing, because frequently a situation impacts more than one chakra. For example, a person who is experiencing an acidic stomach, causing chronic indigestion, would very likely be dealing with an imbalance in the Solar Plexus Chakra. However, to only treat the Solar Plexus would be doing this person a disservice and would not lead to a deep, lasting healing. It is imperative that we look at the whole picture. In doing that, we might find that behind the stomach distress is anxiety. Since anxiety is an intense feeling, its major area of impact is going to be the Heart Chakra. This chakra then, should also be a target area in whatever healing modalities we choose to implement.

Taking this a step further, let's imagine that the anxiety is caused by problems at work that this individual feels unable to talk about. Circumstances such as these would create an impact on the Throat Chakra, which deals with truth and communication. If the above situation were to then cause obsessive thoughts or endless "mind chatter," the Brow Chakra would become involved. And finally, let's envision the distress reaching a point where this person feels forsaken by God. We now add Crown Chakra imbalance to the picture.

The point I am stressing here is that while one may use the information in this book to develop a healing strategy focused on the primary chakra being stressed in a given situation, don't forget to look deeper for the other layers of the problem and treat all the chakras that may be impacted as well. It is also a good idea to utilize daily practices that balance all of the chakras. This might be daily Reiki or the kind of visualization work described in this book. Well-rounded physical exercise or Yoga is another way of energizing and balancing all of the chakras as well.

A Root Chakra Story

Pamela was experiencing chronic pain in the left knee and the low back. She also complained of having difficulty with concentration. She felt a kind of "spaciness" and would find herself putting bar soap away in the refrigerator or forgetting to add flour to the banana bread mixture. She could not shake her fearful feelings and was always waiting for the "other shoe to drop."

These were definitely signs of Root Chakra (survival) imbalance. The instability, worry, and lack of groundedness were all manifestations of a stressed Root Chakra. Upon closer examination, it was also apparent that her chronic, fearful feelings had caused negative impact on the Heart Chakra, and it would need balancing as well. The problems with knee and low back pain, combined with Pamela recounting in session that she had a history of childhood abuse, made it clear that the emphasis of treatment needed to be on the Root Chakra. While this would be our major focus, attention would also be given to the Heart Chakra.

Pamela began including the color red in her life experience as much as possible. She wore it, she visualized it, she bought red cloth and covered a small table with it. On this table she created an altar. Remember that the purpose of an altar is to serve as a focal point for energy, a kind of "reminder site" that keeps the objective of one's focus always in mind. It doesn't necessarily have anything to do with religion. If it feels more comfortable, you can easily substitute the words focal point for altar. On the altar or focal point, she placed things that were representative of the Root Chakra. She had a small sculpture of an elephant and gemstones that resonate with Root Chakra. The gems she choose were ruby, garnet, carnelian and black onyx. Red apples and roses were included on the altar, as were the aromatherapy fragrances of ginger and pine. She also added a picture depicting Archangel Michael, the Divine Association with this chakra.

In our work in therapy sessions we focused on energetically clearing trauma patterns that related to First Chakra survival issues. We also worked with the fearful feelings she was experiencing in order to address the stresses on the Heart Chakra. In addition, as a way of increasing the energy flow to the Heart Chakra, I had her listening to the music of Mozart and Bach and visualizing herself walking in a green meadow every day.

The pain improved immediately and within a month there was no pain in the knee or low back at all. The fearful thoughts subsided and Pamela became adept at choosing to turn her thoughts to those that were more positive and productive. With this shift also came the ability to concentrate and focus more clearly. Daily visualization, which centered on energizing and balancing all of the chakras, was also incorporated to create a maintenance program that would preserve her present state of health.

A Sacral Chakra Story

John, an older businessman was having problems with sexual disinterest, impotence and financial issues. He was feeling isolated and unable to access creative solutions to his business problems. He was also overeating and gaining weight.

It was clear that his primary issues were related to Sacral Chakra (creativity, sexuality, and relationships), so while maintaining practices that energized all his chakras, such as his morning visualization work, we emphasized energizing and balancing the Sacral Chakra. Since color work is so easy for most people, we began with having him visualize and wear the color orange. John was an active, physical sort of person, so we chose processes and activities for chakra balancing that appealed to his active nature. Water is the element of this chakra so we had him swimming, floating and relaxing in water as much as possible. On a daily basis he would gently massage the reflexology point on his foot that relates to the Second Chakra. He carried a piece of carnelian in his pocket and would chant "Vam" as he drove to work. He also increased the amount of water he was drinking and began doing sit-ups every day.

While these activities supported energizing and balancing the Second Chakra, in therapy sessions we focused on exploring the archetypal dichotomy that had plagued him all his life. He "ping-ponged" between two emotional extremes. He was either swept up in the exhilaration of feeling like "king of the world" or immersed in the devastation of the self-pitying, lonely martyr. There was no moderate balanced state of existence for him. We also worked on the trauma he experienced in early adolescence due to a mentally ill mother. It was these unreconciled emotional issues that had been causing the chronic stress and depletion of his Second Chakra.

The combination of chakra balancing therapies began to shift John in a very short time. He began feeling more energized and involved in life right away. He was then better able to find creative solutions to his business problems, and his finances improved. This allowed him to feel more powerful and in charge of his life which impacted his sexual functioning in a very positive way. To maintain this improvement, we developed a daily chakra balancing program that could easily be implemented in his busy schedule.

A Solar Plexus Chakra Story

Turner, a lovely 16-year-old with all the advantages, was having constant conflicts with her parents. She was showing signs of low self-esteem, even though she was beautiful and accomplished in many areas. She was also experiencing digestive problems, shyness, and anxiety regarding decision-making.

While the emphasis of the problems pointed to Solar Plexus Chakra (personal power) imbalance, it was also clear to me that, due to her age and social/sexual development, there was a strong likelihood that there was Second Chakra (sexuality and relationships) involvement as well. In addition, the shyness and feelings of being "less than" were bound to have created Heart Chakra (feelings) and Throat Chakra (communication) stressors.

We worked with balancing techniques that had appeal to a teenage girl. She had an interest in aromatherapy, so we had her using ylang ylang and mint fragrances on a daily basis while she was doing her homework. She wanted to paint her room and without knowledge of the chakra colors, found herself naturally drawn to painting it bright yellow. I completely supported this choice and encouraged her to visualize a brilliant yellow ball in the center of her stomach as often as possible. In the visualization work she also imagined an orange circle in the abdominal area, a sky blue one in the throat and a green one in the center chest area. This would help address the stressed Throat, Heart and Sacral Chakras. She was interested in Yoga and began taking Yoga classes. She was encouraged to do the Tree, the Cobra Posture and the Bow on a daily basis, as these poses are particularly stimulating to the Solar Plexus Chakra. She loved to ride horses and was encouraged to do so, especially in bright radiant sunlight. This helped balance all of the chakras that we were focusing on; yellow sunlight for Solar Plexus Chakra, blue sky to stimulate the Throat Chakra, and green plant growth for Heart Chakra. We also had her wear an amber pendant and eat more complex carbohydrates to further energize the Solar Plexus Chakra.

In therapy sessions we worked on self-esteem issues, peer pressure, and expression of feelings. We energetically cleared a lot of the feelings of inferiority and inadequacy that plagued her. We used role-play scenarios to instill confidence in her, and we also had her keep a journal of her feelings.

Today all of the issues she arrived with have cleared up. She still works with supportive processes and chakra energizing techniques on a daily basis. Her awareness now is such that she can "self-prescribe" what she needs to do when certain feelings and issues show up in her life. She is functioning optimally in school and has a new zeal for life.

A Heart Chakra Story

Linda came into the office because her ex-husband had died and she needed help with her grief. In addition she had a cough that wouldn't heal and chronic shoulder pain. She held onto resentment and bitterness from the marriage and still experienced difficulty with fears regarding betrayal and loneliness. Verbal expression of her feelings was nearly impossible for her.

This situation was clearly an issue of the Heart Chakra (feelings) being stressed and congested by the emotional issues that had deluged Linda in recent years. The infidelity committed by her alcoholic husband that had led to the break-up of the marriage, was the first assault, and after that the emotional bombardment just kept on coming. She had coped by shutting down. She didn't express her feelings to anyone because she felt like a fool and didn't think anyone would ever understand. While it was quite apparent to me that we had to focus on the Heart Chakra, there was also obvious Throat Chakra (communication) and Solar Plexus Chakra (personal power) involvement.

Linda loved gemstones and was also comfortable sleeping on her back, so I had her purchase inexpensive stones that were particular to these three chakras. (See charts of each chakra.) Each night, guided by her intuition, she would choose one or two stones to place on each of those three chakras. She slept with the stones in place all night.

The energetic resonance of these stones was vibrationally harmonious with each chakra and gave it what it needed for energizing and balancing.

In addition, she immersed herself in the music of Mozart and Bach, ate lots of green leafy vegetables and visualized the colors green and pink often. We had her take walks in the outdoors, which offered the stimulation of blue sky for Throat Chakra, yellow sunlight for Solar Plexus Chakra and green vegetation for Heart Chakra. In addition she used a rose fragrance on a daily basis to energize the Heart Chakra. She regularly chanted "Yam" for the Heart Chakra, "Ham" for the Throat Chakra, and "Ram" for the Solar Plexus Chakra.

In our therapy sessions we explored and energetically cleared her co-dependent behavior patterns, the hurt and feelings of inadequacy that her husband's infidelity had created, and the guilt she felt over having wished him dead in moments of anger. She processed her feelings through role-play and the writing of a "completion letter" to her husband which she read to me, and then burned with the intention of transmuting the energy for healing.

Two months later Linda was noticeably changed in her physical appearance. She had an energy and a sparkle that surprised both of us. She was better able to talk about her feelings and had even gotten involved with a support group in which she regularly shared. She liked the crystal/gemstone work so well that she enlarged her collection, and each night she would intuitively select stones to place on any chakra that seemed to need them. She now begins each day with the simple visualization that is given in this book and often does it again as she is falling asleep at night. She loves feeling empowered by the knowledge and tools she has gained that enable her to impact her emotional and physical health in a positive, proactive way.

A Throat Chakra Story

Laura, a lovely senior in her seventies, sought help because she was tired of never being able to speak up for herself in any situation in her life. If she were in a group of more than two people, she would clam up and hardly be able to make eye contact with anyone. The irony was that she was an excellent writer and had a great deal of wisdom and life experience to share. When she did talk in a one-on-one setting, she was interesting and people would enjoy hearing what she had to say, but as a rule she just wasn't confident enough to let herself speak in a larger setting. She also had chronic congestion in her throat and difficulty with her teeth.

It was quite evident that Throat Chakra (communication) imbalance was at the base of these problems. However, upon closer examination, it could be seen that the Brow Chakra (intuition and intelligence) had also become stressed through her chronic thinking that everyone was better than she and would never have interest in her ideas. This was further complicated by her deep-rooted belief that people always judged her. That belief and her long-standing feelings of disempowerment and low self-esteem contributed to Solar Plexus imbalance. In addition, the on-going fear and anxiety she experienced had created a stressed Heart Chakra. One could see that there was treatment needed on many levels with a definite emphasis on the Throat Chakra.

In our joint creation of a treatment strategy, we decided that in order to strengthen and energize every chakra, a visualization exercise would be implemented at the beginning of each day. Using a technique that Doreen Virtue (*Chakra Clearing*) developed, Laura visualized herself in outer space in a dark starry sky. Before her would appear a giant grid of color: red for the Root Chakra, orange for the Sacral Chakra, yellow for the Solar Plexus Chakra, green for the Heart Chakra, sky blue for the Throat Chakra, indigo blue for the Brow Chakra, and violet for the Crown Chakra. In turn, beginning with the red grid, she would visualize herself flying through the grid over and over, allowing the color to cleanse and energize each chakra. This is a powerful technique and a great way to start each day.

Because Laura felt that the verbal freeze-up was the most problematic issue, we worked with many techniques emphasizing the Throat Chakra, but we also kept the Brow Chakra, the Heart Chakra and the Solar Plexus in mind as we decided what processes and tools to use.

She liked aromatherapy, and used fragrances that impacted all of the identified chakras. She particularly liked to combine aromatherapy with her visualization work. Music particular to the chakras on which we were working was used during visualization as well. Since exercising was part of her daily routine, she added to her workout the upper abdominal curl (standing for ease), and the spinal twist for the Solar Plexus, shoulder rolls and back stroke for the Heart Chakra, shoulder shrugs for the Throat Chakra, and eye exercises for the Brow Chakra. She wore a turquoise choker every day and chanted the sounds of the chakras while doing her daily activities.

In therapy we focused on clearing the issues that had contributed to the creation of this "shut down" pattern. We energetically cleared the traumatic issues created in childhood from being teased and shamed for expressing her unusual, creative ideas. These traumatic experiences had blocked the Throat Chakra long ago. We also worked with self-expression and role-play to enhance the level of her confidence so she would be better able to summon her courage and speak up when she wanted to.

I can best summarize her dramatic healing by telling you the story of something that happened to her within six months of beginning our work. Laura made a bold decision to go to a women's conference where she knew only one other person. At the conference she especially loved the daily event in which women went up on stage and told their personal stories to an audience of approximately five hundred women. From the first day she found herself longing to go up there but was sure she could never do it. She managed to express this desire in her daily small group meeting. To her surprise, the other members responded very enthusiastically, thinking it was a great idea and that, of course, she should and could do it.

Armed with that love and encouragement and the newly found strength and confidence our work had created, she was ready to experience a life-changing event. On day three of the conference, with the support of one of her small group members, she walked up onto the stage, told her story, and received a standing ovation. Need I say more?

A Brow Chakra Story

Joshua was an eleven-year-old boy who had recently started having unexplained nightmares. He was terrified to sleep in his own bed and had begun sleeping in his parents' room in a sleeping bag on the floor. He was getting frequent headaches and seemed to always have nasal congestion. His grades in school were starting to fall because he said he just couldn't keep his mind on what the teacher was saying. As he talked to me at the first session, I noticed that his foot never stopped its nervous tapping. He was very worried that all these things were going wrong because he had been the victim of alien abduction. His anxiety level was high because he had developed an unexplainable fear that he or someone in his family might be attacked and hurt or killed by aliens or bad people.

While many of Joshua's symptoms were indicative of Brow Chakra (intuition and intellect) stress, I was also concerned with the stress on the Root Chakra (survival) and the Heart Chakra (feelings). It was clear that we would need to deal with the fearful thoughts and the origin of his nightmares by engaging Joshua in processes that energized and balanced the Brow Chakra. We would also need to address the Root Chakra and Heart Chakra issues that were apparent.

As Joshua was a child, we had to have him doing things that were highly engaging or we would never hold his interest long enough to see any results.

Visualization is powerful for the Brow Chakra, and I knew that being an imaginative child, he would enjoy this kind of process. I gave him several visualization exercises like flying through the color grid in outer space that was mentioned before. I had him seeing himself diving into pools of vibrantly colored water and riding on the back of an elephant (Root Chakra animal) through fields of brilliant red flowers and giant redwood trees. He visualized himself soaring on the back of an owl through the starry indigo blue skies of night (Brow Chakra color and animal). In addition, we started him working on a coin collection. This put him in daily contact with lead, copper and silver, the metals that resonated with the chakras on which we were working.

As the weather was warm, he was allowed to have a "star-gazing" time with his Dad each night. While star-gazing they would do eye exercises focusing on objects first near then far. This is very balancing for the Brow Chakra. During the star-gazing much was being done for all three chakras. Michael was in direct contact with the earth (Root Chakra), he was surrounded by indigo (the Brow Chakra color), and he was experiencing the positive feelings of connection with his Dad, which made him feel safe and also generated great energy for the Heart Chakra. In addition, his mother was encouraged to feed him a protein rich diet with lots of green leafy vegetables. This addressed the Root and Heart Chakras.

The last part of the treatment plan was to introduce Joshua to Archangel Michael, the "heavenly bouncer." Michael is the celestial warrior, the ultimate protector. He is also the Archangel of the Root Chakra. We created a visualization wherein Joshua would call on Michael to show up with his sword and shield whenever Joshua was afraid. He was told that he could sleep with Michael's protective wings around him, if he desired, and Michael was always posted at the bedroom door at night before the light went out. In addition, a picture of Michael went on his nightstand. From the first night this liaison was created, Joshua was able to sleep in his own room. He got very connected to Michael and began enlisting his aid with homework, social situations, and other areas of his life.

Joshua began to lose the fearfulness almost as quickly as he had attained it. The night fears subsided, and he began to be more comfortable talking to his parents and to me about other fears and sources of anxiety. His relationships with his peers and his school work took a little longer to improve but have definitely moved steadily upward. Confidence and security have replaced fearfulness and anxiety. He got very interested in coins and is still collecting them. The result of this work is a child moving in an upward direction with a significantly improved ability to handle the challenges of his world. In order to maintain this improvement, he still engages in the daily chakra balancing activity of flying through the color grids, as well as working with his coin collection.

A Crown Chakra Story

Katrina, a woman in her mid-fifties, came into the session in a terrible state of depression. While she had dealt with bouts of depression before, this time she was having trouble "shaking it." In addition, she had begun feeling emotionally abandoned by her husband and had become totally apathetic about her sexual relationship with him. She had begun drinking excessively and was having so much difficulty functioning at work that she had taken a leave of absence. She felt that she was in a crisis, yet had little motivation or real desire to do anything that would change it.

I immediately saw that she was dealing with Crown Chakra (spiritual connection) imbalance, which goes hand in hand with severe depression. While this seemed to be the core issue, the feelings of abandonment, sexual apathy, and excessive drinking that had resulted, made it clear that the Sacral Chakra (sexuality, pleasure and relationships) and the Solar Plexus Chakra (personal power) also needed addressing. Because Katrina was in such a depressed state, the processes she would implement in an effort to balance these chakras, had to be administered in very small doses.

We began with just having her chant the Seed sounds of each of those three chakras: "vam" for the Sacral Chakra, "ram" for the Solar Plexus Chakra, and "ngngng" (as in sing) for the Crown Chakra. She did this whenever she felt able to throughout the day. This was work she could do lying in bed or sitting on the sofa, so I felt confident that she would follow through. Slowly we added visualization work, which appealed to her, as she was spending a great deal of her time day dreaming anyway. Now at least she could feel that she was doing something productive during that indulgence.

As she had a lot of magazines in her home, when her energy got a little stronger, I had her make color collages of pictures containing orange, yellow, and violet objects. We were now incorporating two of the most powerful chakra energizers: color and sound. We expanded that into the wearing of clothes in those same colors and the planting of flowers in her garden that were orange, violet and yellow. Slowly but surely her energy level and sparkle began to improve. In therapy we focused on processing and energetically clearing her issues of low self-esteem and abandonment.

We included her husband in the work, and once he realized that her condition was not his fault, he became quite supportive of our efforts. He purchased some new CDs for her with flowing "New Age" music that energized Sacral and Crown Chakras. He also bought Beethoven for the Solar Plexus Chakra. He started engaging in nurturing activities that weren't sexually demanding, like foot massages and drawing her candle-lit baths. These behaviors assuaged her fears that he didn't care and allowed her to feel physical pleasure. As her condition improved, yoga was added. This is an excellent way to balance the chakras and increase the flow of energy in the physical body. As these improvements took place, a decrease in the amount of alcohol intake naturally followed. Katrina had not been a true alcoholic; she was just a depressed woman who had been trying, in any way she could, to ease her pain. As her trust and confidence in her husband's love grew, she began to show renewed interest in sexual connection. He refrained from being demanding or critical and instead was gentle and reassuring. This was extremely helpful to the development of feelings of safety and self-confidence.

Today she is back at work functioning well. She comes in once a month for a "tune-up" she calls it. She has renewed zeal for life and a lightness of spirit that would not have seemed possible. She has incorporated daily chakra balancing practices into her life to be proactive about maintaining optimal body/mind health.

Chapter Twelve

Newly
Emerging
Chakras

NEWLY EMERGING CHAKRAS

For thousands of years the principal chakras of the Human Energy System have been the Magnificent Seven with whom you are now well acquainted. Of course, we were aware that there were secondary chakras...many of them. But the primary chakras addressed in energy healing, balancing, and transformation have traditionally been the seven that originally came to us from the Sanskrit teachings. For centuries these awesome wheels of light have served as a series of "step-down transformers" that make it possible for subtle energies to be properly integrated into the cellular matrix of the human system. They have allowed varying vibrational characteristics to come into the body and influence behavior on both the cellular and organismic levels. And as we have seen throughout this book, they have also played a critical role in the regulation of various states of consciousness.

In the latter part of the last millennium, however, new energies have come to the planet, and they have opened up other chakras. I could not complete this book without at least a brief introduction to the newest members of this amazing system. The bulk of this overview will concern the Thymus Chakra, because at the present time, it is of special importance for the peaceful evolution of mankind.

Soul Star Chakra

The first chakra we will discuss is probably the one that has enjoyed the highest level of public awareness. It is often included in diagrams of the chakras that have been used for quite some time, yet it is still rarely included in therapies or bodies of knowledge that address the major chakras. This chakra is called the Soul Star or the Halo Chakra. It is located six to twelve inches above the head. It is the seat of time and timelessness, karma, and portals in and through this time/space continuum. Soul genes, templates, personal archetypes and symbols reside here. It is the source of past knowledge and karmic memory. The Soul Star is said to sparkle and twinkle with a golden hue and resonates with Cosmic Truth and love for others.

An open, responsive, peaceful mind and mental silence are required for this chakra to be fully activated. It brings in wisdom, exultation, illumination and Christ-like qualities. Love radiates from its golden hue. It seems to interact with the Crown Chakra as a kind of transmitter/receiver for communication with other dimensions of consciousness and reality. It is fully activated and sparkling brightly during meditation, when one is communicating with one's God-Self. It is also activated by acts of service, when one is counseling or bringing warmth, nurturing, engaging in compassion, inspiration, and other deeds of kindness to one's fellow man. This chakra is the energy source of the Master Teacher, teaching through grace, expressing the soul's beauty in words, thoughts and communications. It is the portal for divine inspiration and brilliant ideas manifested from our higher self, the Creator, and divine beings. It allows us a clearer connection with higher dimensional Beings, enabling us to channel guidance without going into deep trance.

The Soul Star is the source of the energy of creation, change, and master plans. Old concepts, programmed belief systems, and linear-based concepts are transmuted through this chakra. The Soul Star seems to have the exceptional ability to discern which entities or pieces of information are in alignment with our integrity and only allows those through. Therefore, the higher and clearer our integrity, the higher and clearer the information and guidance we will receive.

Crystals that assist in balancing this chakra are aquamarine, amber, amethyst, diamond, sugilite, yellow sapphire, and tiger-eye.

Earth Star Chakra

At the opposite end of the spectrum is the Earth Star Chakra, which is located one and a half to four feet beneath the feet. It is the grounding chakra and the source of daily life energy, as well as cleansing energy. It is the seat of daily life information. In harmony with its namesake Earth; it resonates with the right to create. It relates to earth tones: brown, black, mauve, and russet. This chakra should be developed simultaneously with the Soul Star.

The crystals that resonate with the Earth Star Chakra are obsidian, Apache tears, smokey quartz and clear quartz.

Well of Dreams Chakra

This chakra is also referred to as the Zeal Point Chakra and the Mouth of God. It is said to be blessed by Buddha and is located at the back of the head at the base of the skull (the medulla oblongata). It is an ancient chakra that is now in a vestigial stage. It reawakens the dreamer in all of us and is the origin of prophetic dreams and visions. It is usually fully activated only in prophetic dreamers and clairvoyants but is becoming activated in more and more of us at this time. When it is fully energized, it will regulate multi-dimensional telepathic communication. It is also said to be important in dissolving the veil between the third and fourth dimensions. Through this chakra, those who are able can peek into the past or the future.

Tension in the neck and upper shoulders can signify an opening of this chakra. If this should be the case, stay alert to visions, new insights, and use the ability responsibly.

The qualities of this chakra are strength, protection, gentleness and gracefulness. This chakra resonates to the color magenta. The crystals that resonate with the Well of Dreams are clear quartz and pink tourmaline.

The Diaphragm Chakra

The Diaphragm Chakra is a little chakra with a big job. It is like a body-mind-spirit, pollution filter. This chakra is located in the region of the physical diaphragm, just under the lungs, above the solar plexus. It assists us in processing many of our base emotions like anger, fear, sorrow, regret, and anxiety. It detoxifies the emotional body, releasing negative, painful emotions. It also clears and releases old traumas from this life and past lives. It detoxifies the liver and gall bladder on physical and emotional levels and brings out issues buried deep within them. This chakra assists in emotional therapy and recovery. It protects against psychic attack and the negativity of other people. One of its most important functions is its role in aiding communication and harmony between the lower chakras

(Solar Plexus, Sacral and Root) and the upper chakras (Heart, Thymus, Throat, Brow and Crown). These groups of chakras differ primarily in the way they process negative emotions: the heart and higher chakras encouraging a more cosmic, loving perspective, and the Solar Plexus and lower chakras, holding onto negatively based emotions and patterns through ego perspectives. When this dissention is unassisted by the work of the Diaphragm Chakra, one is reactive to circumstances rather than having the ability to see the unlimited choices available at all times. When the assistance of the Diaphragm Chakra is present, however, a more harmonious, productive interaction will prevail.

The Diaphragm Chakra is a kind of integrity monitor. It lets you know when you have jumped the track and does its best to get you back on it. When we behave in a way that is not in alignment with our integrity, we build a wall between the self and the ideal vision of the self. It is the Diaphragm Chakra that knocks that wall down by processing the base emotions that derailed us in the first place. It assists us in discerning between that which is important and the "small stuff," while encouraging us to deal with what we must, in order to prevent build-up. When this center is open and clear, you feel free and self-accepting. There is a feeling that you are a being who belongs in the Universe. Conversely, when this chakra is closed or congested, you feel weighted down, isolated and alienated.

This chakra also assists us in developing our 'thought-form body', the ability to bring our thoughts to direct manifestation on the physical level...the idea conveyed in sayings such as "think it and be it" and "what is seen in the mind becomes instantly manifest."

The Diaphragm Chakra works hard when processing and releasing fearful, negative thoughts. You might notice a shortness of breath or tightness in that area when it is working. This can be eased by deep, circular breathing.

This chakra resonates to the colors green and black. The crystals that assist in energizing and balancing it are malachite and aventurine.

THE THYMUS CHAKRA

The Thymus Chakra, which is also referred to as the High Heart, Soul Seat, or Unified Heart, is in my opinion the most significant of the newly emerging chakras. This is a result of its importance in assisting us to experience unconditional love for all of humankind. It is critical to the evolution of an attitude of peaceful, loving acceptance of all people and all beliefs. This chakra is a very powerful energy channel that links us to the earth and to the heavens. This is the chakra of peace and connection, of attunement and alignment with all that is spiritual. As the Heart Chakra is the seat of personal love, the Thymus Chakra is the seat of joy and unconditional love for all of humanity. When the Thymus Chakra is open, we are able to receive love and give it joyfully to the masses. Its influence allows us to care about and connect with billions of other people, creating a web of connection that has not been possible before.

It is positioned above the physical thymus gland, between the Heart and Throat Chakras, creating a pull of both energies. The combination of these energies enables a powerful opening to occur that allows a loving communication between Human and Spirit. This makes it possible for true guidance to easily flow through. It also enables loving communication to move out to the many people who are experiencing fear, threat, and denial of the changes coming to the Earth and the physical body. Only through loving communication can this be done effectively and harmlessly.

The Thymus Chakra deals with many things; specifically with communication with angels, masters, guides, our Higher Self and higher energies from the realms of light. It allows us to access the sacred records. It is an activator of higher consciousness, yet it allows the Higher Mind to meet the Inner Child. It is able to bring belief and spiritual wisdom down from the heavens while keeping us connected to the earth plane.

This chakra acts as a converter and filter for the higher vibrational energies, which are electrostatic in nature. It converts and filters them into electromagnetic energy, which is what we are composed of and what we can assimilate. The emergence of this chakra is directly related to the changes in vibration and frequency that have occurred as a result of the fourth and fifth dimensions moving into the third. The Thymus Chakra enables us to properly integrate and embody these higher, more power-ful vibrations to make them usable.

The Thymus Chakra is the seat of compassion, empathy, joy, peace, serenity, patience, balanced emotions and unconditional love for those that are close to you as well as all of humanity. It is a vortex that pulls in the Christ and Kwan Yin energies, bringing great awareness to the emotional and spiritual planes.

It is the outer doorway for the inner spiritual center, referred to as the Soul Seat, the source of meaning, direction and spiritual longing in life. Among its other functions, the Thymus Chakra also has a large influence on telepathic ability. It strengthens concentration and connects us to freedom of expression and open communication. It assists in the development of confidence, verbal skills, serenity, and spiritual bonding. It opens the Heart Center for giving and receiving and governs our ability to be at peace with ourselves.

The Thymus Chakra bolsters and balances the immune system and brings about healing and wisdom on the mental, physical, emotional, and spiritual levels. Through it, we can ask to be connected to Source and to the power of radiant, healing energy to use for the good of all. It allows us to flow with health, love and ease through times of change and heightened vibrations. Because of the Thymus Chakra's ability to help us deal with upheaval and change, it is of particular importance to people who are healing addictive behaviors.

It is said that the Thymus Chakra was planned at the time of creation but held until we were ready for its wondrous gifts. Some say that the Thymus Chakra looks like the planet Saturn with a solid core of energy and three rings surrounding it. Each of these rings has a specific purpose. The first opens up the channel that enables loving communication between Mankind and Spirit so that true guidance can be received easily. The second ring acts as a filter and converter to make the electrostatic energy of the fourth dimension more easily acceptable to the human system, converting it into electromagnetic energy, which can be stored in the body for healing and self-transformation. The third ring has the ability to resonate with the power of the Solar Plexus Chakra and the Brow Chakra to enable telepathic communication. There is a final ring that is not visible clairvoyantly unless one is ready for, or preparing to, make the initiation into the energy of the Kundalini for enlightenment. This ring connects with the energy of the First and Second Chakras on the low end, and the Crown on the high end, to start the movement of Kundalini energy upward.

Other people who see the chakras clairvoyantly vary in their descriptions of the way this chakra looks. There are those who describe the Thymus Chakra as a binary star, two points of light, separate but touching, merging and working together. Others see it as a two-petaled lotus flower, more in keeping with the traditional Sanskrit descriptions.

If you are experiencing tightness or fullness in the high-heart area, or if you are chronically feeling stressed in the upper back and shoulders, it may be that you are being called upon to open up to the energies of the Thymus Chakra. It would be a good idea to first make sure that you have no physical causes for these symptoms, but once sure that you are in good health, there are several things you can do if you are desirous of activating this charka.

Visualize light coming down from the heavens through the Crown into the Thymus Center. See this center filter and convert this light into energy that flows throughout the whole body to be stored for healing and energizing. See the Thymus Chakra in its full aquamarine glory. See it positioned between the heart and throat and meditate on it growing brighter and brighter and more and more fully energized.

Another thing you can do is the Thymus Thump. Bring the fingertips of one hand together and gently thump the thymus area in the 1-2-3 rhythm of your choosing. Remember to breathe fully and deeply. This is also a great way to re-energize yourself when you are feeling tired. Another cleansing/energizing technique that is very effective is to brush the area about two to three inches above your thymus in an upward direction. As you do this, affirm that you are a clear vessel and that you allow only the highest and best to impact and influence you.

The colors that resonate with the Thymus Chakra are: pink, blue, green, gold, turquoise and aquamarine. The crystals that are important to balancing, healing and energizing this chakra are: aquamarine, apophyllite, blue tourmaline, celestite, clear quartz, crysophase, rainbow moonstone, turquoise and zircon.

In the following section you will find a chart on the Thymus Chakra that is similar to those given for each of the Magnificent Seven. In some areas the information was not known, so you will not find it listed. As with the other chakras, use the information given to create your own strategy for healing, clearing, balancing, and expanding this chakra.

The Thymus Chakra
The Right to Unity with All That Is – "I connect"

Sanskrit Name	not known
Location	Between Throat and Heart Chakras
Gland/Hormone	Thymus
Predominant Colors	Turquoise, aquamarine, blue-green
Archetypes	Humanitarian/Narcissist
Divine Association	Christ Archangel Aquariel Archangel Michael Kwan Yin
Associated Deities	
Hindu	not known
Other	Hina
Sacramental Association	not known
Sacred Truth	*Love one another.*
Qualities	Authenticity Acceptance Balanced Emotions

Qualities (cont'd.)	Compassion
	Confidence
	Empathy
	Joy
	Patience
	Peace
	Self-identity
	Serenity
	Spiritual Bonding
	Sympathy
	Unconditional love
Element and Ruling Planet	Electromagnetic energy Pluto
Developmental Age and Life Lessons	No age Interconnectedness
Seed Sound	Hul (as in "dull")
Vowel Sound	not known
Note	F#
Music	Healing, soothing music
Associated Sense	Hearing
Emotion	Universal Love
Gemstones	Apophylite
	Aquamarine
	Blue Tourmaline
	Celestite

Gemstones (cont'd.)	Clear Quartz
	Crysophase
	Rainbow Moonstone
	Turquoise
	Zircon
Force	Magnetic Attraction
Metal	Platinum
Fragrances	Sage
Herbs for Incense	Sage
Flower	Tea Tree/Pink Manuka
Essential Oils (Aromatherapy)	Pink Manuka
Astrological Association	Pisces
Animals	Dolphin
Foods	Water
Cord in Thymus Chakra Means	"I need you to feel connected."

Function: The Power of Connection

❖ It is known as the High Heart, Soul Seat or Unified Heart Chakra. It is the seat of joy, peace, compassion, empathy, and universal love for humanity. It governs our ability to be at peace with, and accepting of, ourselves and others. It's our connection to world soul, a vortex, pulling in the Christ and Kwan Yin energies. It is a link between Earth and the Heavens.

❖ It is the activator of higher consciousness. It is the outer doorway for the inner spiritual center referred to as the "Soul Seat," which is the source of meaning, direction, and spiritual longing in life. It is the chakra of peace, connection, attunement and alignment with all that is spiritual.

❖ It enables a loving communication between human and spirit, which allows true guidance to flow easily. It specifically concerns communication with Angels, Masters, Guides, the higher self and higher energies from the realms of light. It also has a large influence on our telepathic ability.

❖ It bolsters and balances the immune system. Brings about healing and wisdom on the mental, emotional, physical and spiritual levels. It is the connector to healing energies from Source.

❖ It acts as a converter/filter for higher vibrational energies.

Energy Connection to the Mental/Emotional Body

This chakra resonates to our need for connection with others and with Spirit. It is the etheric heart in which compassion, inner peace, and the web of connection between all people originates. When it is fully activated one is able to give and receive joy and unconditional love to all of humanity. It also aids in opening awareness to the truth of one's existence and in bringing belief and spiritual wisdom down from the heavens (the Higher Mind meets the Inner Child.)

When Energy is Balanced:

You are open to contact with higher spiritual levels. You aspire to love the Divine as well as having selfless love for those around you. There is stability of thought that defines the emotional coloring. Your physical body is strong and healthy. You have increased ability to heal yourself and others. You are emotionally balanced, joyful, loving, well adjusted and capable of effective social interaction.

When Energy is Unbalanced:

You may be stuck in ego, feeling judgmental, self-righteous, and uncompassionate. You stubbornly see only the ordinary side of life. You are unable to discern what your purpose is, and life appears meaningless and empty. You have negative, destructive, impure thoughts and are unable to move through your own boundaries and limitations.

You can also be so open to higher levels, that you lose your grounding on the practical, mundane level. You indulge in spiritual platitudes and ignore the needs of others. You reject and are fearful of, higher spiritual realities.

Energy Connection to the Physical Body

Heart, thymus gland, upper chest, shoulders, throat, breasts, and immune system.

Health Issues

These are not clearly known a this time. However, since the Thymus Chakra is critical to proper functioning of the immune system, it is quite likely that all disease has connection to imbalance within this chakra.

CONCLUSION

I have endeavored to introduce you to the Magnificent Seven Chakras of the human energy system, to open up within you the sense of wonder and awe that I experience when studying and working with them. I sought to give you tools to energize and heal the chakras so that they could function optimally and serve you more fully. I also made an effort to give you a glimpse of the newest members of this expanding system, to allow you to see the evolutionary progression of these amazing vessels of light.

My hope is that you will feel motivated to take a more active role in the health of body, mind, and spirit through consciously working with the chakras on a daily basis. I highly recommend that you set an intention to begin and end your day with focused attention to the chakras. This can be as simple as a five minute visualization, three minutes of chanting the chakra sounds, or a more involved approach that utilizes several of the chakra balancing techniques.

There is very little that need be done to keep these wheels of light shining brightly, and I assure you that all efforts put forth will generate great rewards in the form of abundant health, optimal life-functioning, and the ability to manifest positive life changes.

I wish you joy and blessings in this undertaking. It has been an amazing journey for me and those I have traveled with, a journey of personal empowerment and transformational healing, of health and well-being.

Every journey begins with a single step. Taking that step is now up to you.

BIBLIOGRAPHY

Clinton, Nahoma. *Matrix Work Manual.* Energy Revolution Press, 1999.

Diemer, Deedre. *The ABC's of Chakra Therapy.* Samuel Weiser Inc., 1995, 1998.

Eden, Donna w/Feinstein, David. *Energy Medicine.* Jeremy P. Tarcher/ Putnam, 1999.

Judith, Anodea. *Wheels of Light.* Llewellyn Publications, 1992.

Khalsa, Darma Singh and Cameron, Stauth. *Meditation as Medicine.* Pocket Books, 2001.

Legion of Light. *Chakra Awareness Guide.*

Lehr, Carol and Levy, Susan. *Your Body Can Talk: How to Use Simple Muscle Testing to Learn What Your Body Needs.* Hohn Press, 1996.

Myss, Caroline. *Anatomy of the Spirit.* Crown Publishers Inc.,1996.

Shapiro, Debbie. *Your Body Speaks Your Mind.* The Crossing Press, 1997.

Simpson, Liz. *The Book of Chakra Healing.* Sterling Publishing Co., 1999.

Virtue, Doreen. *Chakra Clearing.* Hay House, 1998.

Wauters, Ambika. *Healing with the Energy of the Chakras.* The Crossing Press, 1996.

Wauters, Ambika. *Chakras and their Archetypes.* The Crossing Press, 1997.

Wordsworth, Chloe. *Holographic Repatterning Manual, Meridian-Chakra Systems,* 1995.

Index

About The Author

Paula Shaw, CADC, DCEP is a therapist, author and renowned speaker. Traditionally trained with a degree in Education and Communications, from Long Beach State University, Paula earned her graduate counseling credentials from Loyola Marymount University, specializing in alcohol and drug counseling as well as grief and loss work. In 1999, Paula fell in love with the newly emerging field of Energy Psychology and its effectiveness in producing rapid results for individuals dealing with the difficulties of life.

Fueled by her newly found passion for Mind/Body work, Paula became one of the founding members of the Association for Comprehensive Energy Psychology (ACEP) and today serves on its board. She developed Conscious Healing and Repatterning Therapy (CHART), in 2000 and introduced it at the first International Energy Psychology Conference .

Paula's desire to learn even more compelled her to explore the world of the Chakras. While yoga students and teachers have been conscious of the value of balancing the chakra system, Paula helped contribute to bringing awareness to the masses with the completion of the first edition of *Chakras: The Magnificent Seven*, which was released in 2002.

Paula now turns her focus to the importance of dealing with loss and life transitions in her second book, *Turn Your Frown Upside Down,* which will be released in the Spring of 2014.

In her 22 years of experience Paula has become passionately committed to empowering clients to help themselves out of pain and into joy. To that end, she gives them what she calls 'tools to go,' which are processes that can be easily learned and implemented anytime, anywhere. Paula is trained in the most effective modalities of the Energy Psychology compendium and is also a Reiki master. She has a private practice in Encinitas, CA. where she serves as Energy Psychology Counseling Specialist with Dr. Andrea Cole at the Center for Age Management.

In addition to her counseling, Paula lectures, writes and teaches a variety of workshops within her fields of expertise, and has been a featured speaker at several ACEP conferences over the years.

A perfect blend of talent, gifts and tools, Paula uses both head and heart to help clients release the sadness and move on to have vibrant lives. Her primary goal is always, to help individuals take control of their lives and turn their dreams into realities.

Web Site: www.paulashaw.com
E-mail: paulashawcounseling@gmail.com

Coming Soon,
Don't Miss Paula's next book!

Turn Your Frown Upside Down

7 Simple Steps to Guide You Though Loss and Life Transitions

Enjoy this free Chapter from the book and check

PaulaShaw.com for the release date in

Spring 2014.

Turn Your Frown Upside Down
7 Simple Steps to Guide You Through Life's Transitions

Chapter 1

The Energy Of Change and Transitions

From the moment we lose the tranquility of the womb and enter the confusion and upheaval of birth, loss and change are part of our lives. Since the normal, human response to loss and change is usually discomfort, is it any wonder that a baby's first act is to cry?

A possession, a partner, a place, an image of self, a sense of security...suddenly gone, creates change, transition, and the inevitable discomfort of the unfamiliar. Even when we are looking forward to a change or transition, such as marriage, it still comes coupled with loss (loss of independence, loss of focus on ourselves etc.) and loss creates discomfort and emotional pain. We often call that pain grief, but that word is really more of a genre than an emotion. Grief comes in many flavors and sizes. It can show up as unstoppable tears, exhaustion or anxiety, fear or reclusiveness. It can manifest as an inability to focus, or an unexplainable, pervasive sadness. It can morph itself into addiction to sugar, alcohol, drugs, cigarettes or food. These are just a few of the possible addictive substances and experiences that can emerge as grief in disguise. And grief, my friends, just like change, is an inevitable part of life.

Sound discouraging? It doesn't have to. Remember the mission of this book; **Turn Your Frown Upside Down**. This book is about shifting, about movement in the direction that will eventually take you back to joy. A life transition doesn't have to be a life sentence of pain, but it does takes deliberate, committed action to find the way out of the painful imprisonment that can become your reality when you are going through difficult times.

The obvious next question would be, *"What kind of action do we take?"* It's a good question and the sad truth is that most people don't know the answer. They have no idea what to do. They don't teach this in school. So how do we know what kinds of actions are productive and which are destructive? Most people learn from watching others and sadly, what they observe are often dysfunctional, unproductive ways of handling change and feelings of loss.

A good deal of the time, people don't even realize that they are experiencing emotional pain unless something very obvious, like the death of someone they loved, has occurred. They don't realize that their depression, anxiety, eating disorder, alcoholism, inability to maintain relationships etc…is very likely the result of pain that originated from a life transition they experienced and didn't come to peace with.

Whether it is the loss of your mother, your best friend, your favorite ring or your job, it's a loss…and loss and change create emotional pain. But what I have found to be true in my twenty-two years of helping hundreds of people, is that when people do have good tools and they get them out and use them, it becomes possible for their pain to transcend and become transformative, insightful and growth-full. That's what I want to see happen for you as you read this book.

Today we are fortunate to have proven, cutting-edge, mind/body approaches that can help people heal far more rapidly and productively than ever before. I have used these tools multitudes of times in seemingly hopeless situations and watched them transform lives over and over again. In this book I will share 7 Simple Steps that include actions and processes to assist you in walking through the pain and discomfort that naturally occur when going through life transitions.

Let me share an example of how finding a root cause, combined with the use of powerful tools, created a life-changing transformation, with one of my clients whom I will call Lynn. She telephoned me after being in bed for days over the break-up of her relationship of three years. She was the CEO of a large, successful company and was now rendered completely unable to function.

She lamented to me that she was devastated, couldn't eat, didn't seem to care about anything and even said she felt like she wanted to die. Lynn exclaimed that she had broken up with men before and never had a reaction like the one she was having. She even confided in me that she was more functional after the death of her mother.

After talking for a bit, I began to see that the recent breakup had triggered an old wound, which had been created by sexual abuse from a trusted family member. This betrayal had set up a belief in her that she would always be betrayed by men she loved. Like so many abused children, she had no opportunity to get help to process and heal the betrayal. Later, other experiences of betrayal in adolescence and adulthood cemented the negative belief even further.

When she fell in love with the man in question, she thought all the betrayal was behind her. Because she was so happy, she let her guard down and trusted him. Imagine the devastation she felt when she found out that he had cheated on her and although he said it meant nothing to him, it meant everything to her. Once more the belief that she would always be betrayed by men had reared its ugly head and she now felt doomed to live this nightmare over and over. This was the core of what had paralyzed her with emotional pain.

Through using some of the mind/body tools that I will introduce to you, she was able to neutralize the betrayal belief, which was central to her devastation. Robbed of its power, this belief was no longer able to drain her energy and zap her hope. Nor was it able to attract life experience that validated its accuracy.

If we openly express painful feelings from the onset of the loss, eventually, the intensity dulls and healing begins. But few of us allow ourselves this natural progression. We have lives. We have things to do and we can't let anything stop us. So we find a way to either access what we think is the fast track through the emotional pain, or we try to avoid it all together.

It's our dread, shame and avoidance of these intense feelings that actually enables them to grow, become complicated and linger. If it were only possible, from day one, to have a guarantee that if we followed our natural instincts to scream, cry, wail and agonize in disbelief, we would heal more rapidly; more of us would do what we actually need to do. But instead we push away the feelings, put on the "I'm fine" face, and try to carry on bravely as if our world hadn't just been blown apart.

Unfortunately, most westerners don't really believe that the outward expression of our devastation will help us heal. Our culture, our family beliefs, our religious training and the messages we get from watching other people, tend to push us in the opposite direction. Instead of feeling our pain, moving toward and through it, we avoid it like the plague. We put on our "stiff upper lips," our "game faces," and use every means available to arrest, deny, alter and submerge the pain that is ravaging our hearts and souls. This denial of our true emotional condition, only serves to provide the ample time and fertile soil required to allow the unexpressed feelings to fester and grow into disease and dysfunction. This author believes that underneath ALL disease and dysfunction is unresolved, unhealed emotional pain.

Why are we so afraid to experience our pain? I believe it's because we have no idea how to deal with it, so we fear that if we open the door, even a crack, we will be helplessly engulfed in it. Feeling powerless and impotent is not a state that we humans are comfortable with, so we tend to move instead, to fear and avoidance.

It is the goal of my work to help people accept and experience their normal, natural responses to pain and stop trying to hide and disguise them. All humans experience discomfort and emotional pain when changes in their life circumstances are not to their liking. But going into fear and avoidance does not serve us. In our feeble attempts to 'set our feelings aside until a more convenient time,' we do ourselves a major disservice and hinder our healing. In fact we set ourselves up for creating more complex diseases and dysfunctional behaviors.

As a member of the Center for Age Management medical practice in San Diego, California, my colleague Dr. Andrea Cole and I both consider health to be a balancing act that involves the body and the mind. When Dr. Cole refers someone to me who is dealing with both physical and emotional issues, the first thing I do is what I call "Excavation Work." The client and I review life experiences and I look for the life transitions, losses and subsequent unhealed emotional pain that inevitably occurred. More often than not, the loss occurred long ago, but went unrecognized and unaddressed. This unhealed emotional pain, sets up the perfect 'Petri-dish' environment in which to grow the components of illness and emotional dysfunction. My friends and colleagues Drs. George Pratt and Peter Lambrou refer to these experiences as *micro-traumas* in their best-selling book **Code To Joy**. In agreement, I must say that I have never seen some level of traumatic circumstances fail to be present in physical and emotional illness, especially in the presence of conditions like cancer and auto-immune problems.

The Body/Mind Connection

The understanding of this mental/emotional/physical connection had its beginning over 2000 years ago. There are ancient writings connecting powerful emotions like anger, grief and sadness with illness. But more recently in the 1970's, O. Carl Simonton M.D. published and spoke prolifically on the connection between grief and the onset of cancer. In the majority of the patients studied, cancer was linked with a significant loss experienced 6 months to a year before the cancer appeared.

Dr. Elilda Evans published, *A Psychological Study of Cancer* (1926) in which she reported that in an analysis of one hundred cancer patients, the majority of those patients had lost an important emotional relationship before the onset of the disease. She saw such patients as people who had invested their identity in one individual, object or role, rather than developing their own individuality. When the object or role was threatened or removed, such patients were thrown back on themselves, with few internal resources to cope.

In *The Type C Connection,* the association between cancer and repressed emotions is further explored. "Primary emotions like anger, fear, and sadness do not have any harmful effect on our bodies. They alter our physiology, but so does every natural biological function. It's only when we <u>habitually block feelings</u> that they become <u>'toxic' states </u>that are closely associated with <u>weakened immunity</u>." —Lydia Temoshak Ph.D. & Henry Dreker, *The Type C Connection.*

Another perspective is offered by Dr. Candace Pert Ph.D. "My research has shown me that when emotions are expressed—which is to say that the bio-chemicals that are substrate of emotion are flowing freely—all systems are united and whole. When emotions are repressed, denied, not allowed to be whatever they may be, our network pathways get blocked, stopping the flow of the vital feel-good, unifying chemicals that run both our biology and our behavior." --Candace Pert, Ph.D., *Molecules of Emotion*

The Body/Mind Solution

Clearly, the current research is supporting the body-mind connection. So doesn't it make perfect sense that a body-mind problem needs a body-mind solution? Quantum Physics has taught us that "Everything is Energy!" That means everything, your thoughts, your behaviors, your skin, your hair…it's all energy. What better way to heal damaged energy patterns than with energy medicine?

The miraculous tools that have been created in energy medicine can help even devastated grievers shift to a place where they can begin to take healing steps and implement healing behaviors into their lifestyles. It is imperative that we explore and employ successful methods from this field when dealing with loss and life transitions because loss is ubiquitous and when it goes undetected and unhealed, both body and mind become endangered. There is no escaping it; life transitions and loss go hand in hand but loss and illness don't have to become inseparable companions.

The Buddha warned us long ago, he said, "Life is suffering," but I think what he really meant was, life is full of change and change embodies loss and when we don't know how to deal with loss, we suffer. Emotional pain can be grueling when we have no tools for dealing with the devastating feelings it generates; feelings such as anguish, anger, hopelessness and a terrifying loss of control. These feelings are difficult and frightening. No one wants to go through this kind of agony, yet we must feel it and walk through it...not avoid it, if we are to heal productively.

My goal is to give you tools and processes to manage and lessen your pain, so you will be better able to walk through your life transitions in a growth-full, enlightened way.

The word *emotion* actually comes from the Latin root meaning "to move." Could it be any clearer? The very name of the thing is telling us how to deal with it. We are to move through our pain-ful feelings, not become them!

It is so tempting to wish we could bypass experiencing and moving through life's agonies. God knows that many people try to do this through the distractions of work, substances or addictive behaviors, but avoiding pain doesn't dissipate the energy of it. If we aren't willing to experience the pain and process through it, we are opening the door to problems. Unhealed emotional pain can linger like a low-grade fever, waiting for some unknown event to ignite it into a fiery, inferno, or, it can become stealth-like, lurking beneath the surface, wreaking havoc from the inside out, through the mechanisms of physical or emotional illness. Fortunately, or unfortunately, in the words of the old saying, "the only way out, is through."

But weathering the shock and devastation of life transitions doesn't have to be a lonely, tortuous walk down a frightening, dark hallway that never seems to end. There are ways to shorten and brighten that hallway, to turn the heavy energy of loss back into vibrant energy for life. Impossible as that may feel now, it can be done. That's what this book is all about. So if you are open to the possibility...let me show you 7 Simple Steps that can help you Turn Your Frown Upside Down.

)96